Police on a Pedestal

RESPONSIBLE POLICING IN A CULTURE OF WORSHIP

Terrell Carter

 PRAEGER™

An Imprint of ABC-CLIO, LLC

Santa Barbara, California • Denver, Colorado

Library of Congress Cataloging-in-Publication Data

Names: Carter, Terrell Writer on policing, author.
Title: Police on a pedestal : responsible policing in a culture of worship / Terrell Carter.
Description: Santa Barbara : Praeger, [2019] | Includes bibliographical references and
    index. | Identifiers: LCCN 2019002252 (print) | LCCN 2019018335 (ebook) |
    ISBN 9781440866371 (ebook) | ISBN 9781440866364 (hard copy : alk. paper)
Subjects: LCSH: Police. | Police psychology.
Classification: LCC HV7921 (ebook) | LCC HV7921 .C337 2019 (print) |
    DDC 363.2/32—dc23
LC record available at https://lccn.loc.gov/2019002252

ISBN: 978-1-4408-6636-4 (print)
        978-1-4408-6637-1 (ebook)

23 22 21 20 19   1 2 3 4 5

This book is also available as an eBook.

Praeger
An Imprint of ABC-CLIO, LLC

ABC-CLIO, LLC
147 Castilian Drive
Santa Barbara, California 93117
www.abc-clio.com

This book is printed on acid-free paper ∞

Manufactured in the United States of America

This book is dedicated to multiple groups:

The families who have lost loved ones to a criminal justice system that doesn't see or acknowledge their humanity;

The police officers who work in a system that asks them to lay aside their own humanity and to ignore that of others;

The police academy recruits that I graduated with in 1997, as well as the officers of the St. Louis Metropolitan Police Department whom I worked with in the 3rd, 6th, and 2nd Districts. I think about you and pray for your safety and sanity on a daily basis. I hope for health, protection, and wisdom as you do a job that only a few are capable of doing.

And to Genevieve and Jerry Carter, for life more abundantly.

Contents

Introduction

"Until the lion learns how to write, every story will glorify the hunter."
—African proverb

When was the last time you experienced the euphoria of a person telling a good story? Storytelling can be a beneficial part of life and can serve multiple functions. Through stories we share information, relate and preserve personal and communal history, encourage people to take specific actions related to a common goal, entertain ourselves and others, and potentially influence the opinions of others. At its best, storytelling can help people become allies around a common cause or, at its worst, create enemies where there had previously been none.

While I was a cadet in the St. Louis Metropolitan Police Academy, I learned that, at its core, policing is primarily about storytelling. One of my academy instructors told us that when we finally began to patrol the mean streets of St. Louis, we had to remember that we all possessed the "magic pen." Because we were the officers and the people that we would encounter on the streets were criminals, whatever we wrote in our police reports would be believed by the public, prosecuting attorneys, and judges. It was up to us to tell the stories of what happened in our encounters with criminals in such a way that criminals ultimately got what they deserved.

After graduating from the academy, I quickly learned that the academy instructor wasn't the only person who held that philosophy. It was embedded in how police work was conducted on a daily basis. During my time patrolling the streets and working in a plainclothes narcotics detail, I saw other officers tell stories that would make most creative writing majors envious. I witnessed officers tell stories that sent innocent, and not-so-innocent, people to prison while simultaneously turning the officer into a hero to be admired. Ultimately, I learned that if I wanted to survive as an officer and thrive within the system of policing, I would have to sharpen my storytelling skills. If I was unwilling to do that, I would not be able to move up in the system, and I would likely not be trusted by other officers.

I learned that storytelling by officers served multiple purposes. By telling good stories, an officer could, more often than not, be assured that a circuit attorney or judge would believe their explanation for why a person should have been stopped and needed to be imprisoned. Thus, good storytelling helps improve an officer's arrest and conviction rates. More arrests and higher conviction rates lead to more accolades and awards from superior officers, which is what lays the foundation for future promotions up the ranks or transfers to more desirable work assignments. So good storytelling is the beginning of a good career.

I watched officers harvest the fruits born of good stories. They improved their arrest statistics. They were given more freedom and favored attention by their supervisors. They received awards. They were given opportunities to work overtime or on special task forces. And they were promoted within the department. They also ignored the stories that families tried to share about how their actions were ruining the lives of multiple people and destroying the trust that was needed between citizens and officers. Storytelling at its worst.

The connection between storytelling and policing is not a new phenomenon. Storytelling played an integral part in influencing how policing was shaped and integrated into our identity as a burgeoning nation. The history of policing in the United States partially begins with the story that certain people needed to be protected against other people.

> The birth and development of the American police can be traced to a multitude of historical, legal and political-economic conditions. The institution of slavery and the control of minorities, however, were two of the more formidable historic features of American society shaping early policing. Slave patrols and Night Watches, which later became modern police departments, were both designed to control the behaviors of minorities. (Kappeler 2014)

As whites sought to explore and inhabit the new world of North America, they believed they needed protection from "savage" Native Americans in the Midwest who couldn't, or wouldn't, recognize God's desire for whites to overtake this new land. After the savage natives were sufficiently under control, African Americans, whether enslaved or freed, were marked for police control. This ever-growing need to control minority cultures was one of the contributing factors that led to the expansion of police and their powers as our nation continued to grow.

Over time, the purpose of policing in America transformed from protecting settlers against Native Americans and protecting slaveowners' rights, to continuing to invest in the acquisition of human capital (including the ever-growing process of convict leasing), to eventually mediating disputes between the haves and the have-nots—the elites and working classes—within society.

> [T]hroughout the 19th century and much of the 20th century, the police functioned as "the army of the status quo" . . . Police departments were culti-vated by urban elites and purposed to "control the burgeoning working class in industrializing northeastern cities" . . . Through the end of the 19th century and into the early 20th century, the police continued to focus on "maintaining order [within] working class sections of urban America." (Escobar 1999, 11–12)

Not surprisingly, since business owners were able to pay for police pro-tection, police protected the interests of business owners and managers over the rights of the workers, in effect becoming something akin to a private security force for those who could afford to secure their services. The services elites requested from police were the kind that ensured the better sensibilities of the elites wouldn't be frustrated by people from the lower classes. "Police patrolled city streets picking up drunks, jailing vagrants, and, if not suppressing vice, at least making it invisible to ensure that the refuse of industrialized society did not disrupt the lives of the more gen-teel classes. On a more sinister level, police acted as the willing pawns of factory owners and chambers of commerce in suppressing labor unions, radical political organizations, and other expressions of working-class sen-timent" (Escobar 1999, 11).

Although the history of policing in the United States partially began from the desire of certain people to be protected from other people, police and the elite have not been the only willing participants in the overall process of storytelling that is policing. Multiple groups that are involved in the pro-cess of policing (white citizens, political officials, media, and the justice system) have a vested interest in shaping and reinforcing the stories that are told. Understanding what kind of story each group is telling, and why they are telling it, can help us gain a better grasp on the overall system of policing in the twenty-first century.

STORIES TOLD BY THE DOMINANT POPULATION

In general, white citizens' stories about policing revolve around a long-held fear and distrust of minorities, especially those who invade their space. Some may disagree with this statement, but its truth is evidenced by a few things. First, the election of a president whose primary plank in his politi-cal platform was the promise to build physical and legal walls to keep out and deport those who, in his mind and in the minds of his supporters as measured by deed and rhetoric, did not "deserve" to be allowed into our country. This fear tactic served him well and led to him being elected as the leader of the world's greatest nation.

Second, this long-held distrust is evidenced by the proliferation of incidents of white people calling police on blacks because they didn't think the black person should be in their community or space. These types of interactions are the outgrowth of social and political beliefs mentioned earlier that whites must be protected from those who are "other." This long-held fear and distrust of minorities makes it easier for whites to turn over more power to law enforcement as long as law enforcement protects their interests as it relates to interactions with minorities.

> Whether whites care to admit it or not, they have a selfish interest in maintaining the categorical mechanisms that perpetuate racial stratification. As a result, when pushed by the federal government to end overt discriminatory practices, they are likely to innovate new and more subtle ways to maintain their privileged position in society. . . . As discrimination moved underground, new mechanisms for exclusion were built into the criminal justice system for African Americans. (Massey 2007, 54)

STORIES TOLD BY POLITICAL OFFICIALS

Political officials tell whatever story they believe will best serve their attempts to get elected to public office. As I will show, they tell stories about crime and criminality in order to influence public opinion for their purposes. They tell stories that exaggerate crime and criminality and who is likely to be a criminal or experience the effects of criminal behavior. These stories also define what criminal behavior does and doesn't look like.

Actions that are indulged in by one group of people can be overwhelmingly understandable, if not acceptable, but when a different group of people with slightly darker skin engages in the same behavior, their actions are unacceptable and categorized as criminal. These politicians have developed an ever-increasing, yet continually marginalizing, vocabulary that clearly delineates between who is good and who isn't, who belongs in certain areas and who doesn't, and whose actions should be looked at with suspicion and whose actions shouldn't.

> Scholars have discovered a typical vocabulary that political contenders employ as they try to construct or ward off problems. This vocabulary includes claims about the causes of problems, how severe their effects are, how frequent or prevalent they are, the social groups they most affect, and the solutions that would best address them. Competing claims about causality, severity, incidence, affected populations, and solutions lie at the core of most struggles to define public problems. Those who wish to construct public problems out of troubling social conditions generally portray those conditions as widespread, as affecting large and diverse populations, or as harming groups that are positively stereotyped, such as children, or

"hard-working Americans." They also seek to present troubling conditions as the product of identifiable causes that should be addressed through public policy. (Lawrence 2000, 24)

In general, minorities, especially black minorities and the challenges that are experienced within their communities, are regularly offered up as proof that they are unable to manage themselves or their communities and therefore need whites to come in and manage them.

> The existing system is a consequence of publicizing and exploiting crime to further politics, bureaucratic organizational demands, and media popularity. It is also a mechanism for controlling and repressing a large percentage of the U.S. population that is unemployed and for the foreseeable future unemployable. The fact that this unemployable population is predominantly African American also both reinforces and expresses the ubiquitous racist ideology of U.S. culture. The imprisonment of large numbers of poor minorities and the shift in emphasis from education and welfare to prisons and criminal justice also hides far more serious harms being done by those in power. (Chambliss 2018, 116)

This is a revolving circle that ultimately ends in multiple self-fulfilling prophecies. Politicians say African Americans from certain neighborhoods are more likely to be criminal due to social influences that come from growing up in poor neighborhoods, although not all African Americans live in poor communities. They cite a lack of stable parental role models as a staple of African American life, although many African Americans, like their white counterparts, come from traditional and nontraditional nuclear families.

These politicians deduce that these assumed truths automatically lead many African American to hold inherent tendencies toward criminality; therefore, society should police that group of people in a way that is different from others. In response to these often-held assumptions, this group is viewed and policed differently than other groups and experiences harsher criminal penalties than other groups. This over-policing and over-penalization lead African Americans to view the system of law enforcement differently and to assume that they will not receive an equitable shake when they interact with any point in that system.

In doing this, the dominant culture is able to keep the minorities "safe" and ensure that the issues experienced in and around the minority group stay in their neighborhoods and do not affect the property values of the neighborhoods of the dominant culture or the reputations of those who inhabit those properties, all the while ensuring that societal issues that reside at a much deeper level are never brought up or adequately addressed.

As we shall see, there is an overabundance of examples of this type of thing occurring. This practice has been in existence from the beginning of our nation's founding and continues today. Although the practice may not look exactly as it did during our nation's formation, it still seeks to accomplish the same goals that were hoped for then: to keep one group of people in subjection to others with the hope of another group experiencing certain economic advantages as a result.

> Keeping a nation focused on street crimes and the myth of young black men as super predators is a smoke screen. It deflects criticism from failed social policies that have not effectively dealt with pressing social issues such as poverty and inequalities in race and class. Instead the victims of these failed policies are blamed for the problems, and increasingly repressive measures directed at the victims are implemented and supported at all levels of government, including police on the streets, politicians, and judges all the way to the U.S. Supreme Court. (Chambliss 2018, 118)

STORIES TOLD BY THE MEDIA

Television media outlets regularly contribute stories that reinforce the idea that whites need to be protected from minorities. As will be shown throughout this book, all sectors of media play their part in keeping the process in motion and ensuring that certain information about the relationship between minorities and police is intentionally filtered before consumption by the public. "The media largely determine what the general public learns about street cops' daily experience with criminals and the underclass, as well as what the middle-class public learns about other groups' experiences with police" (Lawrence 2000, 23).

STORIES TOLD BY REPRESENTATIVES OF THE CRIMINAL JUSTICE SYSTEM

Police and court representatives are the primary storytellers for the criminal justice system. Oftentimes, their stories are colored by a desire to seek advancement and bolster their professional careers. "Law enforcement officers and prosecutors want to get convictions. They may want to further their careers, or they may want to see someone they 'know' is guilty be convicted even if they do not have sufficient evidence to convince a judge or jury. In either case, the need for convictions incites agents to plant evidence, to doctor evidence, and to lie at trials" (Chambliss 2018, 125).

Other times, due to changes in the criminal justice system, law enforcement agencies' stories are colored by the opportunity to reap the monetary benefits of making arrests.

> Local and federal law enforcement agencies today have an even greater incentive to violate the law in pursuit of criminal convictions than in the past. The

property of suspected felons, including people in possession of small amounts of drugs, can be confiscated, and a portion of the value of the property is turned over to the law enforcement agency. (Chambliss 2018, 125–126)

I don't make this statement as any hyperbole. As a former police officer for the city of St. Louis, Missouri, I saw these types of things happen firsthand. Officers regularly faced the temptation to use their police powers to take things away from people who they believed didn't deserve to have them. And they committed those actions under the auspices of "fighting crime." On multiple occasions I witnessed officers arrest someone who didn't need to be arrested and tow their new vehicle because the officer didn't think that person deserved to have that type of new vehicle. "You must be a drug dealer, and no dealer should have a ride better than mine."

I also experienced officers towing vehicles under the false accusation that the owner was a drug dealer for the explicit reason of trying to have this vehicle turned over to the asset forfeiture department. If any officer tried to fight against these types of actions, they were essentially taking their lives into their own hands and would eventually suffer the consequences. White and African American officers alike did these types of things. Officers were rewarded for these actions with promotions and choice tactical assignments. Even the staunchest supporter of police can see the temptations officers face when they interact with people whose voices and stories are less likely to be believed than theirs.

All of these groups (white citizens, political officials, media, and representatives of the criminal justice system) regularly work together, knowingly and unknowingly, to shape the stories that are told about minorities, how those stories are perceived by the general public, and how people interact with minorities when they occupy the spaces they are allowed to operate in. This reality regularly leads to all parties eventually interacting with minorities in a lopsided, and oftentimes nonconsensual, manner.

With the exception of Jimmy Carter, every president since Lyndon Johnson has equated crime with lower-class African Americans. They have become America's modern-day "dangerous class," portrayed as a culture of "welfare queens" breeding criminal children living in a war zone of drugs and guns. Law enforcement agencies have seized the opportunity to ensure their own organizational interests and policies. Crime data are manipulated, and the news media are fed distorted pictures about crime waves, gangs, drugs, drive-by shootings, and a host of other horrific problems. Law enforcement efforts focus on policing the ghetto. The crimes of law enforcement agencies, governments, politicians, and corporations are ignored or relegated to the business pages of the newspaper. Thus, is the crime control industry assured a constant increase in money and power. Like all successful bureaucracies, law enforcement agencies—from the U.S. Department of Justice to rural sheriff's offices—enforce the laws in ways that minimize strain and maximize rewards for the organization. In the day-to-day practice of law enforcement agencies, this translates into enforcing the laws that are violated by the lower classes, minimally enforcing the laws violated by the middle and upper classes, and selectively enforcing the laws that are violated by all social classes—such as using illegal drugs or driving under the influence of alcohol—against the lower classes or treating the transgressions of the middle and upper classes leniently. (Chambliss 2018, 133)

Although we know this is the way that African Americans are typically characterized on television and during election time, those involved in this ongoing process really don't have any incentive to bring about change in the system. If a reality television star can be elected president of the free world based on a platform of calling Mexicans criminal rapists, there really is not incentive to change the rhetoric. Instead, that type of rhetoric becomes the preferred message. If these people most clearly control how, when, and if the story gets told, how can those most affected by the actions of law enforcement and political structures ensure that others hear their story and have the opportunity to at least try to affect the future?

WHAT STORY WILL THIS BOOK TELL?

One thing that can't be overlooked or misunderstood is that the story that is the relationship between African Americans and police is inseparable from the story of how blacks have been treated throughout our nation's history. This relationship has helped to facilitate a view of African Americans and African American life that regularly challenges or removes most semblances of humanity from the African American experience. Through the coming pages, I hope to provide evidence that shows our nation's racially tinged beginnings continue to echo through the system of law enforcement and criminal justice practices today.

Race continues to be one of the primary factors that drives the story of policing in America. It was buried within our earliest laws, nourished through our early communal practices, and continues to bear fruit in the twenty-first century. Unfortunately, the fruit has been a generational story of disparity in how certain groups of people are treated when they interact with police. In general, blacks have a vastly different experience with police than most other minority groups. These stories of disparate treatment shape how entire generations view themselves and the legal system. "In the black community, these narratives are very powerful. You hear them in church; you don't just hear them on the street from kids. . . . Behind every narrative is a culture" (Mentel 2012, 2).

I readily acknowledge that race is but one piece of the puzzle that is the relationship between certain groups of people and law enforcement. I also recognize that for certain groups, race is the primary factor that shapes their relationship with not only law enforcement but also the rest of our nation. Because of race, they are treated certain ways by those who are in power and are not provided access to certain resources by those in power that could drastically improve their communities. We only need to remember the process of redlining that has occurred as it relates to where African Americans can live or obtain loans to purchase real estate.

I recognize that African Americans aren't the only people who have a negative history with law enforcement. I also recognize that they aren't the only people who currently experience tensions related to the criminal justice system. I focus on this group because I am an African American who was raised in a community where most inhabitants had similar experiences with law enforcement. I focus on this group because I have personal experience with negative treatment from police and citizens, both as a civilian and even when I was an active officer.

When I was off-duty, I was subject to the same level of suspicion that any other African American would be. So if an officer didn't believe that I had a reason for being in a particular neighborhood, I would be stopped. They would interact with me like they would with any other suspect, until that officer found out that I, too, had the same job as them. They then would apologize and make excuses for why they decided to interact with me. The same was true for many of the citizens I interacted with. I was subject to the same suspicions many people have about African Americans until they found out I was an officer. After that revelation, I became acceptable to interact with at a more respectable level.

I also focus on this group because as an officer, I saw firsthand how the system of policing targeted African American people and communities as being "less than" and "less worthy" of the protections that their tax dollars, let alone their inherent value as humans, should have afforded them. I left the police department, in part, because I couldn't continue to work within a system that actively treated one group of people better than others.

I recognize that my experiences may not be the same as every other African American person or every African American who has ever donned a police uniform. But based on the stories that I have heard from other officers—both active and retired—the research, testimonials, data, and other information that will be highlighted in the coming pages, I believe that my thoughts and feelings related to policing and how it affects certain communities have not been developed in a vacuum.

Through this book, I hope to help readers who may not be familiar with the historic African American experience with law enforcement understand why the stories African Americans have told over the years about their interactions with police and the criminal justice system, and the general ignoring of those stories by those who could have intervened, has drastically shaped multiple generations' beliefs about law enforcement for the worse. Even after the advent of video technology that is regularly used to legitimize their concerns, African Americans are still accused of exaggerating their experiences with officers or not behaving in ways that would make their interactions with officers go more smoothly. As a whole, whites typically don't have to justify their feelings toward police or deal with the challenges that come with voicing disapproval of police actions. All of this has contributed to the process of people on both sides not trusting each other and solely blaming the "other side" for all the problems that are inherent within the relationship.

HOW DID THE STORY BEGIN?

Although the process of setting Africans apart for separate and unequal treatment began as soon as the first slave ship set sail toward the new world with a fresh cargo of human flesh, scientific- and research-driven efforts to verify the superiority of whites over Africans were kicked into high gear in the 1800s. One of the first tools used in this process was scientific inquiry. In the nineteenth century, scientific inquiry and the "independently" produced data that was accumulated through the study of physical and psychological differences between African Americans and whites were deemed the best tools for determining the superiority of whites and inferiority of African Americans. It didn't matter that those who were conducting the tests and analyzing the data already held the common belief that blacks were inferior to whites and therefore needed to be controlled. The scientific process was used to simply reaffirm what was already believed.

Although this view was not held by everyone, and science alone never served as the defining marker for how blacks should be treated, that would not be the end of the process of publicly determining how inferior African Americans were. When scientific inquiry didn't fully secure the outcomes for how blacks should be treated, a movement arose to use social behavior as a way to discount blacks. "These new scholars of race and society shifted the scientific study of race toward a behaviorist paradigm, measuring inferiority not just by physical differences but also by the historical and contemporary behavior of 'primitive' races in civilized societies. That is, they used evidence of political, economic, and social status found in society to shore up the physical evidence found in the body" (Muhammad 2010, 24).

When this didn't fully work to convince the nation that blacks were unfit to manage themselves, things became even more creative. Anything that could be considered a physical, social, or psychological defect in one black person began to be considered a representation of what was present in the entire group of people. Perceived black criminality became the primary cultural defect that received the most focus. It served as the way to set whites apart from blacks, even though criminal behavior existed at similar levels within both groups. "In all manner of conversations about race—from debates about parenting to education to urban life—black crime statistics are ubiquitous. By the same token, white crime statistics are virtually invisible, except when used to dramatize the excessive criminality of African Americans. Although the statistical language of black criminality often means different things to different people, it is the glue that binds race to crime today as in the past" (Muhammad 2010, 1).

In the end, this strategy was extremely successful in changing the focus of the conversation. In the end, perceived criminality became the defining factor by which the majority of black life would be viewed and white life would not be viewed. I hope the reader can understand the importance of this difference in focus. If I am able to criminalize any of your behaviors while not allowing anyone to focus on any of my behaviors, I have devised a way to tell a story about you and me that will allow me to build and retain power and keep you underneath my thumb without ever really having to fear that you will rise up against me or that someone else will attempt to help you.

Within this book I will tell multiple stories. Stories that are based on my multiple life experiences. Stories based on my experiences growing up as an African American man in St. Louis, Missouri, and living under the shadow of assumptions others had about me and my twin brother that we were criminals in the making simply because of the color of our skin and the neighborhood we grew up in. As a side note, neither of us has ever spent time in jail or prison, we both have completed multiple degrees, and we both are fathers and husbands. And we aren't unique. The vast majority of our family members have experienced the same types of accomplishments.

I will tell stories of my experiences working as a police officer for the St. Louis Metropolitan Police Department. These stories will show how the past and present systems of policing encourage and require officers to perceive and treat African Americans differently from whites based on their skin color and the neighborhood they lived in. I will also tell stories that relate how my religious faith was in regular conflict with my career choices, which eventually led to my resignation from the department, and how I think religious faith or adherence to other systems of belief that value all human life can influence needed changes in the realm of law enforcement and those who may hesitate to question the actions of those who wear police uniforms.

I tell these stories in the hopes of shedding light on a system that typically seeks to protect itself first and inevitably defines itself in relation to how it treats certain people. But at the core, I seek to tell a story about hope.

Hope for reconciliation in relationships that have historically been antagonistic. The kind of hope that is found in a religious text: Psalm 85. As a person of faith, I enjoy reading the Psalms because I appreciate the candor and openness that comes through many of them. There were multiple writers of the Psalms, and each of those writers brought their own personalities, temperaments, hopes, and fears to each poem.

I even appreciate the diverse types of emotions that come through the words of each unique writer—emotion that is based on what they, or a collective people, were experiencing at a unique time within history. Many times, the fact that they were writing from an emotional standpoint caused them to express a greater level of vulnerability and transparency about what they were feeling. This level of vulnerability and transparency caused them to leave everything on the table as they communicated with a power they believed was greater.

Psalm 85 is one such writing that is filled with vulnerability and transparency. In it, the writer reminisces over the past, a time when good things were happening in life, and simultaneously expressed hope for a better future for themselves and the nation they belonged to. We don't know what the problem was that the writer and nation were facing at the time this psalm was written, but apparently, things in their world were not going very well.

As an aside, don't we tend to remember the past as usually being better than the present? I don't say that in a negative way, but when we face challenges in life, we tend to see our current problems or position in life as not being as good as what it had previously been. How many times have you found yourself saying, "If we could just get back to what we used to be!" Or, "Back in the day, things were so much better." This is very relevant for me at the time of this writing because my oldest child recently turned 21 years old, and I must acknowledge that I miss what the past used to be like. I miss the little child that used to be, and as I look at pictures of him when he was a baby and a little boy, all I can think about is what used to be, forgetting about what is today and what can be for him tomorrow.

We don't know what problem Psalm 85 was referring to, but in the writer's mind, things were looking bleak. Whatever the circumstances, the writer pleaded with their Creator to restore their life to the way that it used to be. To have it restored to a time when their Creator's anger was short and forgiving and was pointed somewhere else other than at them. This would be their only hope for a worthwhile future. Their hope could only be found in their Creator restoring them to a prior level of relationship that functioned through love and compassion.

This hope is exemplified in a key word that the psalmist uses multiple times in the passage. It's the word "peace." Others know this word as "shalom." In general everyday use, "shalom" can mean peace, harmony, wholeness, completeness, prosperity, welfare, and tranquility and can be used idiomatically to mean both hello and goodbye. But in the wider, bigger picture of being in relationship with one's Creator, shalom means so much more.

The writer of this psalm is asking their Creator to restore things to the way they "ought to be." For their Creator to allow them to return to a fruitful relationship with their Creator and each other and for their world and life to be made right again. The writer is hoping that things will return to the way they should be, not the way they were. The writer knew that this return to normalcy would only happen if their Creator decided to make it happen or allowed it to happen. That is what the writer's hope is in. That the Creator's love for them would return life to normal. The psalmist can believe this will happen because this has been one of the hallmarks of their relationship with their Creator in the past.

In a sense, this book is my own Psalm 85. It is my attempt to acknowledge that, for multiple reasons, life for certain people isn't all that it could be. One specific reason is due to how this group is broadly perceived and treated based on faulty perceptions about their propensity for criminality. As much as I personally believe in a Creator and hope and intend that that belief will cause me to act in honorable ways toward all people, I readily acknowledge that not all people hold this same type of belief. So this book is my personal call to all who read it to figure out ways to help restore things to the way they "ought to be," not the way they are.

1

The Story of Policing Depends on Who Is Telling the Story

"Since most of us lack direct experience with many social problems, including violent crime, television and newspapers serve as primary, albeit vicarious, sources of information about these issues" (Free 2003, 65).

In order to ensure we understand the story that is being told, we must understand the terminology being used within it. Therefore, we begin digging deep into the story by uncovering the meanings behind a few words and ideas that are used when we talk about law enforcement's interactions with what has become known as black criminality.

Fairness: Whether the justice system's interactions are believed to be just or equitably applied across all intersections of people. "When the justice system is perceived as unfair, untrustworthy, or as failing to respect an individual's group membership, therefore, it will be seen as inadequate and violative of the rights of the group to which an individual belongs" (Peffley and Hurwitz 2010, 30).

Hero: A person who does what the general public is unable or unqualified to do. "To qualify as hero (a person must experience) a degree of personal risk. For example, an individual that returns to a house fire in order to help others get out would be coded as a heroic action. Throwing oneself in the way of a gunman in order to 'take the bullet' would be another example of descriptive language fitting this category" (Frisby 2017, 170–171).

Media Influence: The reality that the vast majority of people get their information, especially information about people who are different from them, primarily through media outlets. The media outlets that they choose to get information from typically only reinforce the beliefs that the viewer/reader already holds. Thus, media doesn't teach people anything new, but instead reinforces current prejudices. "It is not inconsequential that individuals in the United States report that the majority of the information that they receive about crime and criminals comes from the media" (Oliver 2003, 4).

Police Legitimacy: Whether an officer's interactions and attitudes are believed to be just or equitably applied across all intersections of people. Although an action may be legal or lawful, it may not be considered legitimate by any given community. Public opinion concerning the legitimacy of any police action may vary based upon the community in which that police action has occurred. If an officer or department has a history or reputation for interacting with members of a given community in a negative way, the legitimacy of any action will likely be questioned.

Proactive Policing (often referred to as "Real Policing" by law enforcement officials): The work conducted by police when they intentionally pursue misdemeanor and felony arrests. "A variety of activities, often positively associated with field interrogations, traffic stops, and/or enforcing laws related to driving under the influence, loitering, or possession and public consumption of drugs and alcohol" (Way and Patten 2013, 4).

The key to proactive policing is that proactive officers typically "are not following a specific crime reduction strategy as devised by the administration but are simply contacting 'suspicious' people and trying to catch would-be lawbreakers. This is also what officers in some jurisdictions call 'hunting' and is almost exclusively practiced concerning visible crimes (for example, possession or selling of drugs, prostitution, and carrying guns; officers informally refer to people engaged in these activities as 'dirtbags' or 'scumbags')" (Way and Patten 2013, 5).

Racialization: Using racial factors as one of the primary ways to determine who is subject to police interaction and how those interactions proceed. "The classification of people into groups by reference to their anatomical features, such as skin color and facial features, and the making of judgments about their innate and cultural attributes and/or social worth based upon those features" (Owusu-Bempah 2016, 26).

Thug/Criminal/Dirtbag: How blacks are publicly described when they interact with law enforcement officials. This definition recognizes the media practice of regularly portraying African Americans in a less-than-positive light. As will be shown in a later section, African Americans are more likely to be shown in a negative light when compared to how whites are portrayed in the media, regardless of the circumstances. For example, whites, no matter the circumstances, will likely be portrayed in a sympathetic light or described using sympathetic language, even if they have been found to have killed someone. Later data will show that even white mass murderers are portrayed in a more positive light than African Americans who have committed less egregious crimes.

Now that we know the terms, we can think about how they are used to shape the stories we hear about policing and black criminality.

STORYTELLING AS A FUNCTION OF THE HERO-MAKING AND VILLAIN IDENTIFICATION PROCESS

Our nation loves heroes. This is evidenced by, among other things, the continuing popularity of comic book superhumans who, unlike us normal human beings, are able to leap tall buildings in a single bound. These heroes are made, and their legacies are secured, through the stories that are told about them in print, through movies, and on television screens. One of the reasons we idolize these fictional characters is, for the most part, they use their powers for good and willingly make sacrifices that typically serve the greater good of humanity. Although the heroes don't necessarily make much money from their actions, those who tell their stories sure do. Some of the most profitable industries in our nation are those that help tell the stories of superheroes through various media.

But superhumans aren't the only people we view as heroes. We view athletes as heroes because of their power and strength. In the past, athletes like Muhammad Ali and Kareem Abdul-Jabbar proved to be as mentally strong as they were athletically competent. They were heroes as much for their mental acumen as for their physical prowess. But they paid a price for their outspokenness on social issues. Today, athletes like Lebron James and Colin Kaepernick leverage their celebrity to bring attention to multiple social causes and are handsomely rewarded for their outspokenness.

News makers and news breakers receive the title of hero as well. We admire their work, their tenacity, and the fact that they seem to seek to hold those in power accountable to the common person. There was a time, not too long ago, that newscasters like Walter Cronkite and Tom Brokaw were household names and trusted voices within our nation because they could be trusted to hold politicians' feet to the proverbial fire in hopes of keeping government transparent and focused on serving ordinary citizens.

With the advent of multiple media outlets and innumerable social media methods for immediate information sharing, anyone can become a news maker or news breaker. Although the primary news breakers have traditionally been trained journalists who, ideally, seek to inform our nation of what is occurring and how our lives are affected by certain events, one of the current challenges of this process of potentially anyone making or breaking news is that some people, whether intentionally or unintentionally, see their job as one of the ways to shape public opinion about certain people and groups by attempting to dictate who should be considered a hero and who should not.

But who or what is a hero? Previously, I defined a hero as a person who was able to do something that the general public is unable or unqualified to do. Dr. Scott LaBarge provides a definition that I think adequately clarifies my thoughts when he writes, "The term 'hero' comes from the ancient Greeks. For them, a hero was a mortal who had done something so far beyond the normal scope of human experience that he left an immortal memory behind him when he died, and thus received worship like that due the gods" (LaBarge 2000).

One thing we may not be aware of is that heroes weren't always good guys who lived lives of purity and sacrifice at all times. They also had the ability, and potentially the inclination, to commit certain atrocities that negatively affected others. "[P]eople who had committed unthinkable crimes were also called heroes. . . . Originally, heroes were not necessarily good, but they were always extraordinary; to be a hero was to expand people's sense of what was possible for a human being. What a hero did was more important that their moral composition" (LaBarge 2000). So a hero wasn't determined by how closely a person resembled a Boy Scout. They could experience major moral failures and still be capable of positively affecting other people's lives. Heroes didn't always have to wear white or be a saint.

I wonder if the realization that it's possible that heroes don't always consistently act like the "good guys" will cause any of us to reevaluate what our definition of a hero is and what the implications of this new realization will lead to. This idea of our heroes not being fully perfect may force some of us to reconsider what is acceptable and unacceptable for our heroes to do in their downtime. It may even cause us to reevaluate whether we need heroes in the first place. It may even lead us to ask what happens when our heroes fall short of our expectations for them and whether there should be some type of repercussion when heroes publicly fall.

Despite the moral and ethical conundrums this line of thinking may lead to, hero making fills a necessary vacancy that exists in our collective lives. It helps us identify people that we can look to for help and adoration when we think we can't find similar qualities within ourselves or our acquaintances. We yearn to look up to someone or some group that consistently puts others before themselves. We want to trust in someone who is willing to give more than they take so others' lives can be better. Safer.

We also want someone bigger and better than us to believe in because we think having a hero enhances our lives, makes our society better, and provides us with hope that one day we will be able to relate to others and the world in a different way. "A close examination of cultural myths illuminates how a society describes itself. Joseph Campbell, who studied myth for much of his scholarly life, states that two orders of mythology exist: the spiritual and the sociological. The latter links the individual to a society" (Krause and Smith 2014, 11–12). Even if it isn't true right now, if we try hard enough and long enough, we can one day be like them and make a significant difference for others, eventually being recognized for how little we get in return for how much we give to help others.

What are some of the other general qualities that we find appealing and seek to attribute to our heroes? Dr. Philip Zimbardo has attempted to answer this question in his article "What Makes a Hero?" Dr. Zimbardo describes heroism this way:

> First, it's performed in service to others in need—whether that's a person, group, or community—or in defense of certain ideals. Second, it's engaged in voluntarily, even in military contexts, as heroism remains an act that goes beyond something required by military duty. Third, a heroic act is one performed with recognition of possible risks and costs, be they to one's physical health or personal reputation, in which the actor is willing to accept anticipated sacrifice. Finally, it is performed without external gain anticipated at the time of the act.
>
> Simply put, then, the key to heroism is a concern for other people in need—a concern to defend a moral cause, knowing there is a personal risk, done without expectation of reward. (Zimbardo 2011)

Dr. Zimbardo also notes that although heroes have the potential to do great things for altruistic reasons, that doesn't insulate them from experiencing the desire or impulse to do some not-so-heroic things. Just because a person has heroic qualities or performs heroic acts does not preclude them from doing things we may consider antiheroic. We all possess ideals and attributes that have been shaped by our life circumstances. Those circumstances help direct each of us toward certain viewpoints about life and people. They also shape our desires to either look toward others for heroic acts or to perform heroic acts ourselves.

A final thought by Dr. Zimbardo informs us that the vast majority of people whom we consider heroes don't engage in heroic activity alone. They understand that saving the world or a local community becomes possible when you work alongside others. They save the world through the support and teamwork of others who share a common purpose, as well as common resources. "Heroes are most effective not alone but in a network. It's through forming a network that people have the resources to bring their heroic impulses to life" (Zimbardo 2011).

Although the circumstances that bring a potential hero to the attention of the media may be accidental or come by nontraditional means, the process of making law enforcement into heroes is not. "Most news about policing, just as much news about a variety of social issues, is structurally biased in favor of official sources and culturally biased in favor of officially sanctioned claims" (Lawrence 2000, 49). As will be shown in the coming pages, even when an officer is found to have committed a gross abuse of power on camera, media outlets are still strategic in their attempts to lionize law enforcement and insulate officers from critique and criticism. Media regularly prop law enforcement up as heroes to be envied and protected, sometimes at the cost of truth and community good, and even when information clearly shows they have overreached past decency, legality, and legitimacy through their actions.

This media bias can lead to an unquestioning allegiance to law enforcement by the ordinary citizenry who may not fully understand the history and purpose of policing or the many issues that are present within the current incarnation of police in the United States. This is evidenced when Cleland writes:

> Police officers don't choose what happens in the world, they simply defend us from it.
> Across America, our only defense against the robbers, gunmen and criminals is our law enforcement.
> I can say that I have the utmost respect for those few in blue who do have that bravery and selflessness. (Cleland 2017)

This sounds like hero making to me. As a former officer, I say this without an ounce of hyperbole. Having worked as an officer for the St. Louis Metropolitan Police Department, I can attest to the hero making that occurs through, and because of, this type of thinking. I agree that, in general, many officers don't choose what happens in the world or the areas they patrol. But they do choose how they will respond to the people and circumstances they find themselves interacting with. Unfortunately, some decisions aren't altruistic and are actually selfish because, as I will show, they are built on a need or desire to be perceived as a certain type of officer in order to be promoted, be given choice assignments, or be considered a member of the inner circle so that when something goes terribly wrong, they know they can depend on other officers to help them cover their tracks.

I also understand that, unfortunately, some officers have been killed or seriously injured while performing their police duties. But over the past 20 years, data shows that violence against officers has steadily decreased while complaints about police misconduct have steadily increased. And I personally understand that it takes a certain level of courage to strap on a gun belt and badge every day. But as an officer I was taught that it's easy to be courageous when the largest and most powerful gang in the community all wear the same badges and uniforms.

I recognize that Mr. Cleland's thoughts are not an anomaly or simply the idealistic thoughts of youthful exuberance. A large percentage of whites in America hold to the narrative that all officers are heroes because they voluntarily place themselves in harm's way in order to make our society a better place. They believe the job of a typical rank-and-file police officer is increasingly dangerous. The general public sees officers as involuntary combatants in an ongoing street war that seeks to make police into primary casualties. Radley Balko demonstrates the fallacy in Mr. Cleland's line of thinking when compared to the current reality of policing. Balko points out, "According to FBI statistics, 27 police officers were feloniously killed in 2013, the lowest raw number in more than 50 years. (The previous low was 41 in 2008.)" (Balko 2014). Based on prior statistics collected since the mid-1990s, policing is actually becoming safer, with fewer police being shot or assaulted. I realize that this statement flies in the face of what the media tells us and what police departments hope we believe, but as we will see, the media does everything it can to tell a specific story about police.

Also, although personal gun ownership has risen dramatically in the United States in recent years, violent crimes have decreased, along with a corresponding decrease in violence toward police. Although the militarization of police, as was evidenced during multiple race-based conflicts that have occurred in recent years—for example, in Ferguson, Missouri, after the killing of Michael Brown by a white officer—is believed to be necessary, the instances where a threat against police actually rises to the level where military-type vehicles and weapons are necessary to resolve the conflict are few. Hopefully the reader noticed that I used the word "necessary" instead of the word "preferred." Law enforcement may prefer to use military-style vehicles and weapons as a means to intimidate citizens into submission or compliance, but their use is not mandatory.

For some, the natural response to reading this will be to ask, "Where did the writer get the idea that policing is or isn't so dangerous?" First, we primarily get the idea from media outlets and law enforcement themselves. Before I go too far, I want to make sure to state that, as a former police officer who patrolled two of the busiest and most dangerous districts within the city of St. Louis, Missouri, during its first go-round as the "most dangerous city in the United States," I know that policing can be dangerous and that officers can experience events that most people would never dream of. I also know from personal experience that it only takes one mistake or one momentary loss of concentration on the part of an officer, and they could lose their lives.

But I also recognize that the high-stress, life-threatening experiences that are highlighted in the news and television dramas are primarily fewer and further in between than most civilians know. Most days of patrolling the streets in any given urban metropolitan city or rural county are filled with the mind-numbing monotony and stress of interacting with people who don't seem to know how to handle their day-to-day existence and basic life affairs, drive reasonably, or generally treat others with decency.

I state this, not simply as personal opinion, but as the testimony of the officers that I stay in contact with who regularly apprise me of what policing is like today, as well as officers who have left law enforcement because they felt drained by the mental weight they carried due to what the system of policing requires of officers. These officers' complaints aren't about how dangerous the streets are, although they can be very dangerous at times, but instead are about how difficult it has become to perform police functions in a system that doesn't care about the citizens being patrolled or the officers who patrol the streets and interact with those citizens.

When did this narrative about officers being heroes begin? According to Dan Marcou, it occurred in the 1960s and 1970s as a way to bolster public opinion about officers as they suffered the consequences of trying to protect certain neighborhoods. Marcou also relates that during this time frame, politicians began to use the words "war" and "warfare" to describe policing and its ensuing atmosphere. As much as politicians cared about their constituents, they also cared about their careers. What better way to ensure job security than to scare people into trusting them to fix the communities' problems, even if they didn't live in those communities or regularly visit them? Especially when the problems that were being identified revolved around the growing fear of people who were different from the politicians' constituencies in so many ways. This fear and entrusting to politicians the authority to define this new "war" and modes of "warfare" led to multiple crime commissions and eventually the national "War on Drugs." It also led to the rise of the "warrior cop," the only person qualified to make an impact on crime, especially the kind of crime found in urban (African American) communities.

This narrative continues to be facilitated by the fact that the vast majority of white people don't regularly interact with police. They typically receive their information about police, policing, who participates in committing crimes, how often crime is committed, and where crime is likely to occur through what's shared by the daily news media outlets and talking heads they choose to follow, as well as from fictional television programming. The problem with this is the media can't always be trusted to accurately portray information about crime. "It is well documented that both print media and television—including drama, news, soap operas, and cartoons—all greatly exaggerate the incidence of crime in the United States, particularly violent crime" (Free 2003, 65).

One of the problems that is inherent in having this limited opportunity to learn about other people who may be different from you, as well as only getting information from a source that likely already shares your political and social leanings, is that it is unlikely your beliefs or preconceived ideas about someone will be challenged. Instead, they will likely only be verified. A person is less likely to question how people who are different from them are portrayed and simply believe what is said about them by their preferred media outlet, whether that outlet is conservative or liberal.

An additional problem with a person receiving the majority of their information about people who are different from them from one type of source is that the portrayals of those different people may be intended to be satirical, but the viewer considers them accurate and assumes that the opposing group of people is truly like that. When they are confronted with a person from that group who doesn't fit their preconceived ideas, they are likely to believe that person is the exception to their expectations and not an adequate representation of what their people must be like.

Because of this lack of personal experience with police and criminality, the general citizen likely believes what they are told by these media programs. As Americans typically spend less time interacting with people who are different from them and instead learn about different cultures, groups of people, and what police do from watching them on television or finding information about them through Google and YouTube videos, it becomes easier to understand why people's view of police and policing may not be adequately informed.

> Heavy viewers of television gave higher estimates of crime rates, overestimated the number of men with a job in law enforcement (as the demography of the television world is full of law enforcement officers), and had been influenced in their perceptions of police procedures and crime characteristics. Generally, heavy viewers also seem to see the world as a more dangerous place. Television fiction appears to have a significant impact on people's perception of crime, the police, and police work. (Bulck 2002, 116)

This narrative also continues because law enforcement personnel have made it a priority to actively frame and/or participate in the story that is told about them. I don't blame them for this. This is an understandable act of self-preservation. What better way to try to ensure that public opinion surrounding your actions and attitudes is shaped in a way that makes you the hero at every turn? What better way to ensure that the public is sympathetic to you, regardless of the decision you have made and the outcomes that follow that decision? It is more beneficial to frame almost every incident as "us versus them," and whoever "them" is are always the bad guys that need to be dealt with. Officers are never bad guys themselves. They are simply heroes who may have been overzealous in trying to do good.

By attempting to control and influence the stories that are told about them, police organizations hope to insulate the collective body from being held responsible for the actions of a singular officer, especially as it relates to violence perpetrated against citizens by officers. This is evident when an officer's actions have been proven to be over the top, such as an incident of police brutality, and department representatives frame that officer as a lone wolf who acted alone or in a way that didn't represent the overall culture of the department. These representatives and departments never willingly divulge information that clarifies the level of violence that is perpetrated by officers against citizens. Instead, the particular instance is always framed as an anomaly.

Despite the fact that law enforcement is very active in the process of telling and protecting their story, they are not always happy with the results that appear publicly. "Despite the fact that police voices are much more common in the news than those of activists or academics, police generally believe that the news does not fairly represent them" (Lawrence 2000, 49).

WHAT TYPE OF STORY DOES LAW ENFORCEMENT USUALLY TELL ABOUT ITSELF?

Regardless of the type of interaction the system of law enforcement representatives finds itself in, you can rest assured that these representatives want to control the narrative that is being expressed at all costs. One reason for this is that if they are thought to be doing the right thing for the right reasons the majority of the time, they can build goodwill with the general public so that when something does go wrong or someone does something that should be unacceptable, they will have hopefully earned enough respect and goodwill that they can cash in when it's needed.

By actively developing or cultivating a reputation for doing what's right, departments can also require greater subordination from the general population. It's essentially akin to them saying, "If we've been known for doing what's right in the past and having a reputation for being good, then most of the things we ask or require of citizens is due to our desire to do what's right and good. There's no reason to think otherwise." When they, on the off chance, resort to violent or extreme means to obtain compliance from citizens, that extreme action should be excused because it's either out of the ordinary or a citizen forced the officer to behave in such a manner.

An inherent set of challenges accompanies any person's, entity's, or system's attempts to control how it is defined by others or its attempts to define itself strictly on its own terms and with the vocabulary of its choosing. One of the inherent challenges to this practice is transparency. In order to make sure this type of process is effective, police must control the type, amount, and time frame that citizens receive information about police interactions with citizens.

One of the biggest challenges for departments in this area has been the increased proliferation of cell phones and social media applications that capture and convey how officers interact with citizens at any given moment. Multiple officers have said that cell phones have hindered them from being able to effectively perform their police duties. That should leave anyone who hears that with the question, "What duties do you need to perform that shouldn't be seen by everyone at any given time?"

Overall, this type of process leads to intentional and unintentional consequences related to what the typical citizen is willing and/or capable of learning about police, especially when they typically don't have to interact with police in real life. Due to this type of reality, a person may not see the value in locating and learning new information about how police operate or interact with people who are different from them, or understand how police tactics are developed or implemented in neighborhoods and communities that are different from theirs, and how all of this is framed and shaped by law enforcement in order to gain more support and compliance from the public.

The immediate consequences of the process described earlier are that law enforcement officials use this circular system that they have created as a way to continue to control those whom they are patrolling instead of operating as an equal source of power and/or solutions with that community for the problems that face the community that the circle encompasses. Instead, it seems as if they prefer to have citizens following orders instead of working closely with them on adequate solutions. "In its continual aim of enhancing legitimacy, the police are invested in bolstering *subservience* (subordination to and respect for police power) and *separation* (a sense of police superiority and prestige)" (Herbert 2006, 481).

This line of thinking fosters an attitude by police that they reside and operate above those they are hired to protect and serve, and because, for all intents and purposes, citizens are unable to manage their own lives, it is reasonable for officers to hold certain attitudes toward them. Ultimately, this can lead to officers believing they are the final arbiters who should decide what is right and wrong, who deserves or doesn't deserve mercy, and who will and will not receive due process.

WHAT TYPE OF STORIES DO POLICE TELL ABOUT OTHERS?

Unfortunately, we typically identify our heroes according to how they exist in contrast to certain villains. Every hero needs a villain. Luke Skywalker needed Darth Vader. Superman needed Lex Luthor. Batman needed the Joker. The St. Louis Cardinals need the Chicago Cubs. Hulk Hogan needed Andre the Giant. Villains show the world what power looks like when it is corrupted, what opportunities look like when they are squandered, and how resources are wasted when they fall in the hands of the less worthy.

Who are the biggest enemies of law enforcement? Black males. This is not hyperbole from a writer trying to sell books. In the coming pages, I will show how history and scientific and psychological research data prove this statement to be true. How did black males become the villain that would regularly be contrasted against law enforcement? It began with the intentional process of devaluing and dehumanizing black existence that commenced before America was fully established. By historically dehumanizing this group of people, society is consistently conditioned to expect them to be treated in ways that would not be acceptable for other groups of people to be treated. It also ensures that when that group attempts to speak up about how they are treated, no one will see the need to defend them or accept their complaints.

This process of dehumanization was in practice when Brits traveled to countries where the historic inhabitants had darker skin than their own. They compared these indigenous people to primates and presumed these darker-skinned people were less developed than those with white skin. "Dehumanizing representations of African peoples are nearly as old as Europeans' first contact with West Africa" (Goff et al. 2008, 292). This process continued throughout the travels of British sailors looking for new land for them to inhabit. "Early European maritime writings described primitive people who seemed more closely related to apes than to White explorers. As theories of race moved from theological to biological, the rationale for racial hierarchy relied even more heavily on the 'Negro-ape metaphor'" (Goff et al. 2008, 293–294).

This line of thinking was first established through informal and infrequent interactions between British representatives. Eventually, informal and infrequent meetings began to form the foundation for reasoning that classified itself as intellectual and scientific. "Although this linkage predates scientific racism, it drew increased interest and popularity when Franz Boas, the preeminent anthropologist of his time, and even Charles Darwin, speculated that there might be an evolutionary spectrum among primates containing monkeys and apes at the least evolved end, continuing through savage and/or deformed anthropoids, and culminating with Whites at the other end (as most evolved) Peoples of African descent, therefore, were theorized to reside somewhere between the deformed and the simian" (Goff et al. 2008, 293).

The resulting practice of identifying and perceiving blacks through a lens fit for primates served to greatly influence the general public's perception of black culture and black men. "The 'scientistic' grounding for this representation was used to bolster growing stereotypes that peoples of African descent were innately lazy, aggressive, dim, hypersexual, and in need of benevolent control. It is not surprising, then, that the portrayal of African peoples as apelike became an iconographic representation rivaling even minstrelsy for popularity in visual culture during the 19th and early 20th centuries" (Goff et al. 2008, 293).

The reshaping of black males as apelike and then as villainous within the story that is criminality began as an outgrowth of a political strategy from the South. After successfully legitimizing the practice of comparing blacks to primates, politicians then, over time, shifted the public's focus onto black criminality by making blacks the target, and torment, of standard law enforcement practices. This antagonistic relationship came forth as a political strategy that sought to use black criminality as the means to develop a certain mind-set about crime, how it should be handled and who could handle it, and how to keep white communities safe.

It was best exemplified through the Republican political strategy that eventually became known as the "Southern Strategy." This strategy was essentially the roadmap for framing black criminality for politicians and dealing a substantial blow to the Democratic Party in the South for years to come. The strategy began with discussions about "states' rights" to choose how they dealt with crime. It was argued that individual states should be able to choose how they dealt with their criminal element without the Supreme Court intervening in inappropriate ways.

Over time, the focus broadened to include "states' rights" to deal with how certain entitlement concerns were dealt with, like welfare programs and who could or should participate in them, how to deal with student busing after the Supreme Court's unnecessary intrusion in states' educational systems, access to voting for African Americans, and other affirmative action concerns after more Supreme Court meddling.

The common factor in the strategy was the practice of giving most, if not all, issues a negative face, which meant presenting an African American face as the foundation for whatever problem was being discussed. Strategists knew that giving it an African American face would effectively scare or enrage white constituents. The goal of this political strategy was to appeal to the overwhelming racial concerns of working-class and southern whites and simultaneously deplete the Democratic Party of its teeth.

This political strategy was successfully honed and harnessed by multiple presidents, including Richard Nixon.

President Richard Nixon laid the groundwork for reinstituting some of the racially tinged practices of law enforcement that had previously been outlawed. President Nixon advocated for higher conviction rates. Nixon put the taxpayer's money where his mouth was between 1969 and 1973 by tripling the federal government's law enforcement budget and increasing federal aid to state and local law enforcement agencies from $60 million to nearly $800 million. Unfortunately, much of law enforcement's efforts at reducing crime were targeted at poor and minority communities. (Carter 2019, 34)

Ronald Reagan walked in the path Nixon cleared for future law-and-order presidents. His efforts would have likely made Nixon proud.

In addition to taking on drugs, Reagan was famous for promoting the "black welfare queen" image in America. Historian Duchess Harris wrote, "The welfare queen is the defining social stereotype of the Black woman, a lazy, promiscuous single Black mother living off the dole of society. She poses a threat to the Protestant work ethic that drives America and the American dream of social advancement and acceptability." This sentiment was echoed by James Kilgore, in his book *Understanding Mass Incarceration.* Mr. Kilgore says, "Creating the image of the Welfare Queen as a criminal misuser of taxpayer dollars and perpetuator of sexual immorality helped build the case for reallocating money from social services to law and order." (Carter 2019, 35–36)

Not to be outdone by his mentor, Ronald Reagan, the elder George Bush homed in on the opportunity to use the fear of black men as a plank in his presidential election strategy against Michael Dukakis.

In addition to black women becoming the poster children for welfare reform, black men became the poster children for criminal justice reform. This was most evidenced by the portrayal of convicted criminal Willie Horton. Horton was a convicted felon who, while already serving a life sentence for murder without the possibility of parole, was allowed to participate in a weekend furlough program in Massachusetts where presidential candidate Michael Dukakis served as governor. During the furlough period, Willie Horton committed another string of crimes, including raping a white woman.

Horton and his crimes became the centerpiece of a racially based scare campaign for presidential candidate George H. W. Bush. Dennis Rome, a professor of criminal justice, wrote that due to the tactics used by candidate Bush, "Blacks are the repository for the American fear of crime. Ask anyone, of any race, to picture a criminal, and the image will have a black face. The link between blackness and criminality is routinized by terms such as 'black on black crime' and 'black crime.'" Although public discourse of "black on black" crime is common, there is little talk about "white on white" crime, even though a 2011 report from the Department of Justice said that 84 percent of homicides of whites is by whites. (Carter 2019, 36)

And lest we think that Democrats were impervious to this tactic, it was Bill Clinton who helped to establish the egregious laws that punish drug crimes that are considered black disproportionately when compared to drug crimes that are considered white. Also, Hillary Clinton was the person who famously called the younger generation of black males "super predators."

The result of this overall strategy was that blackness became consistently equated with criminality. If you were black and lived under circumstances that others deemed unacceptable, you were automatically expected to hold criminal tendencies. "A growing body of research demonstrates that people more readily apply racial stereotypes to Blacks who are thought to look more stereotypically Black, compared with Blacks who are thought to look less stereotypically Black" (Eberhardt et al. 2006, 383). And the "blacker" you were (darker skin, broader nose, thicker lips), the more criminal you likely were. "People associate Black physical traits with criminality in particular. The more stereotypically Black a person's physical traits appear to be, the more criminal that person is perceived to be" (Eberhardt et al. 2006, 383).

Although African Americans make up approximately 12% of our nation's population, they represent almost 40% of our nation's prison population. This practice of "anticipated criminality" and the punitively proactive and reactive criminal justice policies currently in practice have effectively led to a steady increase of black males being introduced to some aspect of our nation's prison system, with some estimating that a quarter of African American males will experience a stay behind bars.

I must reiterate that this process didn't come about by accident. It was made possible by politicians' and law enforcement's efforts to criminalize blackness and the things that were in close proximity to it. Since Reconstruction, our legal system has made regular use of laws to minimize the movement and progress of African American culture and opportunity. From laws that made it illegal for African Americans to be in public without an express purpose related to employment, to laws that made it illegal for African Americans to hold certain positions of employment or for whites to employ them in certain positions, or for them to even live in certain areas, the legal system has been used as a tool to protect whites, not just from African Americans but from any population they felt threatened by, and to keep them separate from those they considered "less than."

Researchers have spilled much ink trying to understand and articulate this inherent (a more precise description may be learned) bias that the general public has against black males. Although there is never a complete consensus of opinion as it relates to any given subject, there is much commonality in thinking among social scientists and researchers about how the regular portrayal of black males as criminal in media and by law enforcement affects the general public's perception of that group.

> Researchers have highlighted the robustness and frequency of this stereotypic association by demonstrating its effects on numerous outcome variables, including people's memory for who was holding a deadly razor in a subway scene, people's evaluation of ambiguously aggressive behavior, people's decision to categorize nonweapons as weapons, the speed at which people decide to shoot someone holding a weapon, and the probability that they will shoot at all. Not only is the association between Blacks and crime strong (i.e., consistent and frequent), it also appears to be automatic (i.e., not subject to intentional control). (Tonry 2011, 5)

As I stated earlier, the results of this intentional process have had devastating consequences for black communities in general, and black males in particular. The mere existence of black men leads to them being, at a minimum, consistently perceived as criminal, simply because they bear certain natural features.

> The paradigmatic understanding of the automatic stereotyping process—indeed, the one pursued in all of the research highlighted above—is that the mere presence of a person can lead one to think about the concepts with which that person's social group has become associated. The mere presence of a Black man, for instance, can trigger thoughts that he is violent and criminal. Simply thinking about a Black person renders these concepts more accessible and can lead people to misremember the Black person as the one holding the razor. Merely thinking about Blacks can lead people to evaluate ambiguous behavior as aggressive, to miscategorize harmless objects as weapons, or to shoot quickly, and, at times, inappropriately. (Eberhardt et al. 2004, 876)

I recognize that some would assert that the plight of black males as overrepresented in the criminal justice system is not due to the actions of law enforcement, but solely due to the propensity of black males to be more violent and criminal when compared to the rest of the population. This line of thinking seeks to minimize and overlook the social and legal history that has shaped, controlled, and interpreted black culture through targeted social, political, and legal movements, such as America's War on Drugs.

Through the War on Drugs, a concerted effort was put forth to minimize drug use in America. This effort included bolstering old drug laws, as well as instituting new laws. Unfortunately, the punishments associated with white people's drug use and sales were vastly different from those associated with black people's drug use and sale. For example, penalties for possession of drugs that were consistently considered "white" drugs, such as powder cocaine, were substantially lower than possession of drugs that were consistently considered "African American" drugs, such as crack cocaine. Crack cocaine is simply powder cocaine processed in a particular way. Yet sentencing guidelines for possession of crack cocaine were substantially greater and a person had to essentially be in possession of a pound of powder cocaine in order to receive the same punishment that came with possession of an ounce of crack cocaine.

Within efforts like the War on Drugs, crimes associated with predominantly black communities are further marginalized and dehumanized in ways that crimes that are typically attributed to white communities are not. The crack addiction epidemic of the 1980s and 1990s was viewed as an exceedingly sinful stain on black society and black progress that would only be abated through harsher criminal sentencing for all parties involved. In contrast, the current heroin and opioid epidemic occurring in predominantly white communities is publicly framed by politicians, health professionals, and the media as a public health emergency that will only be fixed through compassion, adequate investment in resources and opportunities, as well as innovative thinking for the greater good. Many in African American communities have been left to wonder where this type of compassion has been for those addicted to drugs within their communities.

The change in tone has been startling, but not unprecedented. A similar process occurred in the 1970s and revolved around the public perception and punishment of the proliferation of marijuana use. "Black people were locked up to attract white votes. When severe policies occasionally hit whites especially hard, as happened in relation to marijuana in the 1970s, the policies were quickly changed. In many parts of the United States, possession of and small-scale trafficking in marijuana were effectively decriminalized" (Tonry 2011, 4).

This change occurred because whites were displeased with their children being locked up and the negative perception it brought toward them and their families. I can imagine these white parents asking, "Why should my child be locked up and carry the social stigma that comes with being arrested for something like drugs when black youth are also using drugs that are probably worse than what my child experimented with?" This intentional reframing of who is criminal and what entails criminal behavior caused President Nixon to rethink his strategy on the War on Drugs. When President Barack Obama pushed for similar efforts, he was accused of being soft on drug crimes. This sense of leniency that is acceptable for white drug crimes is not found when it is perceived that a particular drug is indulged in by primarily black addicts or a particular crime is more often committed by black youths.

This process of showing leniency toward the indiscretions of white youth allowed white parents to, in a sense, make moral and legal judgments about the behaviors of others without having to consider or address whether their own actions should be defined by the same terms as minorities, or whether their indiscretions should be judged according to the same standards they hold for others, or whether their crimes should require the same types of penalties that are given to minorities. This has made it easier to sell the public on the idea that certain behaviors, or certain people that commit certain behaviors, deserve harsher penalties. These types of attitudes and practices have persisted across our history, regardless of who occupies the office of the president.

HOW DOES MEDIA HELP TO PORTRAY BLACKS AS THE WORST VILLAINS?

Data shows that criminality runs across black and white communities at a similar rate, but black criminality is consistently described in harsher terms and reported in ways that continue the process of dehumanizing them, while white criminals are described in ways that try to repair their humanity. This practice remains in place, even when a black person is the victim of a crime at the hands of a white criminal.

> Differences can be found in news media in terms of portrayals of blacks as victims. We find that media rely on different practices when covering crimes involving African Americans, Hispanics, Asians, or Muslims. As suspects, they are quickly characterized as terrorists and thugs motivated purely by evil intent. While white suspects are often described as "lone wolves"—violent acts created by one angry white person. Black victims are often vilified and evidence for that can also be found in news stories. The lives of Black victims in news stories often provide subtle cues that the justification for the murder or shooting are behaviors that they are responsible for. For example, because Trayvon Martin was wearing a hoodie, that behavior was framed in stories as being just as responsible for his death as his shooter. News stories on the Michael Brown shooting often times framed the event around the thought that Brown stole cigars from the convenience store. In other words, in terms of Black victims, media often times frame the event that somehow offers a justification for their deaths. (Frisby 2017, 165)

Although black criminals are described in terms that highlight the level of violence that was perpetrated and the dehumanized qualities they possess, white criminals are described in terms, not of violence, but of their psychological state during the commission of their crimes.

> U.S. media rely on different words and descriptive language when covering crimes involving African Americans or Muslims. For example, after the "Dylann Roof incident," media narrative formed quickly for him in that we read in news stories that Roof probably had some "mental issues and didn't know he had done anything wrong." It seems as if media coverage humanized Roof and referred to him as a sick, victim of mistreatment or inadequate mental health resources. (Frisby 2017, 176)

When was the last time you read a story or observed a news report that tried to humanize a black criminal by describing his life circumstances in a sympathetic manner? When was the last time you heard of a police officer stopping at a fast-food restaurant to purchase food for a black suspect after he committed a violent crime against a white person as the officers who arrested Dylann Roof did?

This tendency of the media to frame white criminality with language addressing mental health concerns and black criminality with dehumanized language was recently explored and quantified by a group of researchers who wanted to better understand and identify the tenets of this media practice. They found that in at least one-third of media coverage relating to white males who conducted a mass shooting—a shooting that involved more than four immediate victims—that the white shooter's actions were framed around mental illness, implying that the shooter's actions were contrary to their natural personality. Only 2 percent of shootings committed by African Americans mentioned the potential of the black shooter having mental illness, effectively framing them primarily as criminals. Researchers determined that media outlets are 95 percent more likely to attribute a white shooter's actions to mental illness than they are an African American's.

Why does this type of media portrayal matter? Because it influences how one group and their actions within our society are viewed sympathetically because of their skin color, whereas another group, who may commit the same crimes although at a much smaller rate, are vilified because their skin tone is sharply different.

> It seems as if media outlets tend to cast the violent acts of White criminals as unfortunate anomalies of circumstance and illness. For Black shooters (and, to a lesser extent, Latino shooters) media outlets render their crimes with a brush of inherent criminality.
>
> This isn't to say that crimes shouldn't be fully examined, and that personal hardships and society don't play a role. But if the circumstances of one group's crimes are being explained in an empathetic way, and another group's crimes aren't given the same level of care and attention, we wonder whether this can insidiously influence how we perceive huge swaths of the population—criminal or not. (Frizzell et al. 2018)

Unfortunately, I think the reality is that African American criminals are being described in terms that seek to make them into worse criminals than those who are white and that black criminals deserve to be more feared and treated more harshly than white criminals. As more data becomes available, I don't have to think this is true. It is a fact that blacks are considered more criminal than whites, and this belief is reinforced throughout much of our society. This belief affects how whites perceive blacks and their propensity to participate in criminal behavior. Both academic research polls and popular opinion polls reveal that when whites think of crime, they think of it in relation to blackness.

When asked what people typically commit more crimes, African Americans are consistently identified. When asked what crimes should receive harsher penalties or punishments, the crimes that whites think more African Americans commit are identified. Other data shows that when whites view news programs on a regular basis, they eventually begin to overestimate their chances of experiencing a crime at the hands of a black person and underestimate their chances of experiencing a crime at the hands of a white person.

HOW DOES THE STORY INFLUENCE WHAT WE THINK IS ACCEPTABLE FOR POLICE TO DO?

Our beliefs about police power are primarily shaped by our personal experiences with both law enforcement and criminality. "[R]acially polarized evaluations of the criminal justice system are based, at least in part, on the radically different experiences of Blacks and Whites with police and the courts—experiences that can be either personal or vicarious" (Peffley and Hurwitz 2010, 29). If we have grown up having had primarily positive experiences and being fed positive imagery about police, we likely will trust them and affirm most of their actions. If we have not grown up with positive experiences or imagery as it relates to minority cultures, we likely will defer to others to tell us how they should be treated.

> Consistent with prior research, race is the strongest predictor of attitudes toward the police and criminal justice agencies. Blacks are more likely than Whites to perceive racial disparities in policing and in the criminal justice system and to report personal experiences of discriminatory police treatment. A substantial proportion of Whites sees these institutions as operating in a colorblind fashion. (Weitzer and Tuch 1999, 502)

Weitzer and Tuch also outline other interesting facts about how race and social class/status affect a person's perception of criminality and how police interact with people:

- Better educated Whites are significantly more likely than less educated Whites to perceive discrimination against Blacks by the larger criminal justice system and by the police in the protection of communities, but they are not more inclined to see police racism as widespread. Irrespective of class position, Whites are more reluctant than Blacks to acknowledge racism in American society, whether in the police or in other institutions.

- Irrespective of income and education, Blacks tend to lack confidence in the ability of the police to treat individuals impartially in their communities.

- Lower-class Black communities are policed more heavily than are middle-class Black communities—largely because of greater law enforcement demands on the police. Individuals living in lower-class Black neighborhoods are thus more likely to come into contact with police officers, increasing the chances of friction in the encounter—friction that participants may define as racially motivated.

- Although residents of middle-class neighborhoods may indeed experience less conflict with police officers in their communities than do their counterparts in lower-class neighborhoods, middle-class status does not appear to insulate Blacks from police behavior that is perceived as discriminatory.

- [M]iddle-class Blacks may indeed have few problems with the police inside their residential neighborhoods, but they may experience more frequent conflicts with the police when they travel outside their neighborhoods—a context where a person's middle-class status is no longer visible to the police. (Weitzer and Tuch 1999, 503)

In the end, personal prejudice is one of the most important factors in determining whether a person is able to recognize the disparity in how white and black criminals are portrayed.

HOW HAS THE STORY THAT'S BEING TOLD SHAPED SOCIETAL BELIEFS ABOUT WHAT'S ACCEPTABLE FOR POLICE TO DO TO BLACK PEOPLE?

The dehumanization of things related to blackness and the humanization of things related to whiteness have led to an ever-widening gap in how the two groups are treated by law enforcement. Data shows that whites receive better treatment, regardless of whether they are the victim or the perpetrator of a crime. Concurrently, blacks receive harsher treatment, even when they are the victim of a crime. Research also shows that when police interact with white victims, they are treated with a high level of respect and compassion. Black victims typically are not. "Relative to crimes involving African-American victims, White victim crimes feature significantly faster police response times, significantly higher probabilities of arrest and prosecution, and more 'vigilant' investigative strategies" (Peffley and Hurwitz 2010, 34).

Some may respond to this data and claim that these findings are overexaggerated because police patrol neighborhoods and communities equally and are professional enough to set any personal prejudices aside as they relate to how they treat victims of crimes. Unfortunately, the data related to that idea shows that this is also a false belief.

Studies by social psychologists show that police officers, like members of the general public, have such a strong association between crime and African Americans that merely thinking about the concept of crime brought Black faces to mind. In addition, merely thinking about Black faces makes it easier for police officers to detect guns and knives when they do not have clear images of these objects. This and other experimental studies suggest that despite training designed to control discriminatory responses, the police and other justice agents often fall prey to a variety of unconscious biases and associations. (Peffley and Hurwitz 2010, 34–35)

These subconscious beliefs consistently come to the surface and are evidenced by the differences in how officers interact with black and white citizens during traffic stops. Through one study that examined recordings of interactions between police and citizens, it was shown that there was a dramatic difference in how police regularly spoke to and interacted with white and black citizens (Voigta 2017). Regardless of the race of the officer or the particular circumstance for the interaction, police were found to regularly disrespect black citizens, while treating white citizens favorably.

The way an officer treats someone during an interaction goes a long way to reaffirming or changing a person's perception of police and how they treat certain groups of people. If an officer shows respect and tact during that interaction, the citizen may not appreciate having to deal with the potential that they or a loved one may have committed an infraction, but they will likely have a positive response to the officer's attitude and professionalism.

Before the reader accuses me of basing my thoughts on the opinions of black people who may have had a bad experience with police here or there, my ideas are based on firsthand experience as an officer, as well as academic studies that have been conducted. Studies such as the one conducted by Voigta only used the words recorded through body cameras worn by police officers. Through this study, he was able to gain data that was shaped by experiences that were initiated and controlled by police officers. From the experiment, Voigta found the following differences in how officers interact with white drivers versus their interactions with black drivers:

- Utterances spoken by officers to white community members score higher in Respect. Officer utterances were also higher in Respect when spoken to older community members and when a citation was issued; Respect was lower in stops where a search was conducted. Officer race did not contribute a significant effect.

- We found that the offense severity was not predictive of officer respect levels and did not substantially change the results described above.

- Officer Respect increased more quickly in interactions with white drivers than in interactions with black drivers.

- Indeed, we find that white community members are 57% more likely to hear an officer say one of the most respectful utterances in our dataset, whereas black community members are 61% more likely to hear an officer say one of the least respectful utterances in our dataset.

- Regardless of cause, we have found that police officers' interactions with blacks tend to be more fraught, not only in terms of disproportionate outcomes (as previous work has shown) but also interpersonally, even when no arrest is made, and no use of force occurs. These disparities

could have adverse downstream effects, as experiences of respect or disrespect in personal interactions with police officers play a central role
in community members' judgments of how procedurally fair the police
are as an institution, as well as the community's willingness to support
or cooperate with the police. (Voigta 2017, 6523–6524)

In addition to the studies I have referenced, I will provide links to other
studies at the end of this book that share data that more clearly delineates
the differences in how officers view and treat black and white citizens.

I will attempt to summarize some of the reasons why there is a vast
void between how African Americans and whites view police and the
criminal justice system and how the two groups of people view life in
America. First, in general, African Americans have a vastly different history with law enforcement and the criminal justice system. Laws have
consistently been used to control African Americans and give whites
advantages over others. These laws have effectively developed a system in
which African Americans have had to reach certain levels of establishment that whites didn't in order to be considered acceptable. Second,
when blacks have complained about treatment by police or the criminal
justice system, historically, whites have told them that their complaints
were not valid, even when there has been quantifiable data or physical
evidence to substantiate their complaints. We continue to see this as officers are regularly not prosecuted for overstepping their boundaries, but
black victims of police action are told they should have complied with officer directions, no matter what those directions are. And finally, we have
made police into heroes who must receive the benefit of the doubt for
almost any decision they make because they sacrificially work a dangerous job that brings little, if any, benefit to the officer.

The story that has been told about black criminality has produced negative effects that blacks will continue to suffer through for the foreseeable
future and that the vast majority of whites likely will summarily dismiss or
simply not comprehend. Until the distance between the lived experiences
of both groups of people has been narrowed, there will continue to exist a
chasm that will be hard to cross.

As this chapter comes to its end, I would like to ask you a question. When
you hear the word "legacy," what comes to mind? I know that sounds like
an odd question to pose, especially due to the subject matter that has been
discussed so far, but please humor me. A simple definition of legacy is a gift
of property, especially personal property, such as money, that's left by a will.
It's a bequest from one person to another. A secondary meaning of legacy
is anything handed down from the past, as from an ancestor or predeces-
sor. Simply put, a legacy is an inheritance that is left to someone from someone who preceded them.

What is the legacy that America has left, or will leave, future generations as it relates to our nation's and law enforcement's perception and interaction with African Americans? As a person of faith, a black man, and a former officer, this question is important to me. As a person of faith, it's personally important because the principles that guide my faith frame legacy as an important thing. The idea of legacy is an important idea in the Bible. In the Hebrew language of the Old Testament, the idea of legacy comes from the word *chalaq* and carries with it the idea of receiving a portion or a share of something.

One of the interesting things about the process of giving and receiving an inheritance in the Bible is the fact that the terms for receiving an inheritance are typically dictated not by the person who receives the gift, but by the person who gives the gift. These terms are usually spelled out in a will or in another written form. I imagine most of us have given thought to the kind of legacy we plan on leaving behind for our loved ones or cherished institutions. Our wills outline what should be done with money that's left behind, jewelry, family heirlooms, and multiple other things that were important to us during our lifetimes.

When one of my grandfathers passed away, he left me his most cherished physical legacy: his library of pastoral and theological books. Although I was happy to receive that treasure trove of books, I really didn't have room for all of them, and truthfully, I didn't agree with the theology of most of those books, so I donated them to other pastors who could use them. Although I was very thankful that my grandfather wanted me to have them, when I received them, I didn't have much use for them.

When my father died unexpectedly of a heart attack in his early fifties, he didn't leave a physical legacy for our family. Although he had a small amount of life insurance, he didn't have any savings or anything else we typically think of as valuable physical legacies to leave his wife or sons. This forced me to think about what I was going to leave behind for my children when I am gone, so I began to plan more intentionally and appropriately.

Although many of our legacies deal with money, land and so on, a legacy can include more than just physical items. A legacy can be nonphysical, like attitudes, dispositions, or ways of thinking about life that are passed from one generation to the next. In that sense, a legacy can be a good thing or a not-so-good thing.

In another religious text, Psalm 78, a writer explores this idea of legacy, but the legacy that is being considered is not a physical one. The text explores what it means to leave a legacy of faith for future generations to follow and what happens when a legacy is not necessarily as faithful as it could be. As is unfortunately the case with so many other psalms, it is believed that Psalm 78 was written during a time when a people who believed they were marked as God's children were not exhibiting as much obedience to their Creator as they should. It was likely written when this collective group was experiencing the fallout from yet again failing to live in a way that clearly reflected their relationship with the One they had been called to follow.

It seems as if the purpose of Psalm 78 was to give a recap of a brief period in Israel's history and to serve as a reminder of the Creator's faithfulness amid Israel's unfaithfulness. In a sense, that's what a legacy is all about, isn't it? To remember someone and the impact or importance they played in our lives. To remember the good things about them and how they positively affected our lives. And how their gift, what they have left to us, will help us to make impactful memories for others in the future.

These ideas of memory, experience, and expectation are on full view within Psalm 78. The writer remembers the glorious deeds that God performed on the behalf of God's children. From calling Abraham out and away from his father and promising to make him into the father of a great nation, to his descendants ultimately becoming a nation unto themselves, the writer of Psalm 78 calls the reader to remember God's act of saving the people from slavery and bondage in Egypt to freeing them and giving them success in reaching the Promised Land. They are encouraged to remember the stories that were passed down, the oral legacies, about how God provided for their every need through miraculous events. How God transformed them from being a weak nation to one that was feared and, for a time, was virtually unstoppable.

The writer encourages them to expect that the Creator would do the same things for them. That God would provide for them in unimaginable ways and lead them over, under, and through any obstacle that they would face. When the people allowed their lives to be guided by these memories of faith fulfilled by God's faithfulness, they would be unstoppable.

Unfortunately, the psalmist reminds the readers that Israel's failures were like those of past generations. Their failures, and the failures of prior generations, were, ironically, related to their memories, experiences, and expectations. Like previous generations, they failed to trust God and to take God at His word. They let what they thought they were seeing dictate what they believed about God's love. They began to see God through the prism of their own actions, instead of through God's actions, and their expectations of God's plan for them were lowered. They let what they wanted for themselves become more important than what God wanted for them. When that happened, life always turned out less then what it should.

What did the writer of this text say his readers needed to do? To remember God's love and faithfulness, to experience God's love and faithfulness through obedience, and to expect God to make life better than we could imagine when we place ourselves under God's loving care. I think that's the point of Psalm 78. To live and leave a legacy of faithfulness for future generations to follow. Don't make the same mistakes as other generations.

Instead, learn from their mistakes and miss out on the heartache and pain of trying to do things our way. Instead, let God dictate what God wants for our lives, because God's plans are always better than ours.

You may be asking what does any of this have to do with a discussion about perceived black criminality or understanding African Americans' distrust of our legal system? Like the readers of that text, we have a conscious choice to make about the legacy we will leave behind. Will it continue to follow the negative path set by prior generations, or will we blaze a new path? Will we continue to create memories of disparity, or will we actively seek to listen to the people who are most harshly affected by the system as they seek to give suggestions for fixing it?

What will the next generation that's watching us say when we're gone? This isn't a theoretical question. It is one that faces us every day, even though we may not be thinking about it. Your children, my children, our grandchildren, and future generations are looking for us to set the example of what beneficial relationships with people who are different from us can look like. Hopefully the reader notices that I haven't said anything about letting crime run rampant or freeing people who have been verified to be a danger to society. I don't advocate letting criminals do whatever it is they want. What I am advocating is that the criminal justice system treats everyone equally/fairly and not assume that just because a person has darker skin or comes from a particular neighborhood that makes them inherently criminal. Multiple other factors contribute to a person committing crime. Those factors regularly cross race, socioeconomic status, and all the other things we use to categorize someone as a menace to society.

2

How Does the State Fit into the Storytelling Process?

"Violence, in the United States, follows a distinct color line that segregates white violence as a matter of maintaining control and protection, and black violence as acts worthy of criminalization and death. Ultimately, this distinction reinforces the stark difference between the importance of white and black lives in America" (Lewandowski 2017, 1).

In the prior chapters, I have established that there is a story that has been told relating to criminality in the United States, why it's told, and the frequency with which it's told. For a few moments, I want to take a more purposeful look at how politicians help tell this story and how they develop and use laws as a way to ensure the story continues to be shaped in a particular manner.

In our democratic society, the job of politicians is to respond to the needs and concerns of their constituents. It seems that currently, the primary concerns of many constituents in America revolve around the desire to develop stronger checks and balances in order to not only keep certain groups or people out of our country but also out of certain local communities. "The existence of significant racial or ethnic minorities in a community is often perceived as an intrinsic threat by the racial or ethnic majority" (Snyder 2013, 8). We want to keep them out primarily due to their race and perceived unworthiness to live near or among us.

As I previously pointed out, this is not a new phenomenon. Our nation's history has been built upon the idea that certain groups of people are inherently more worthy of acceptance and inclusion within the American experiment and the benefits that inclusion brings. "Race undeniably plays a role in determining access to resources and power in American society, and since whites have traditionally enjoyed higher levels of economic prosperity, representation in government and other positions of influence, and more positive health, educational, and occupational outcomes, they are often treated as a privileged and dominant group, with blacks or any non-whites considered non-dominant groups" (Snyder 2013, 8).

It benefits those who want to keep access to the highest levels of the American dream restricted to present minorities as outsiders who either don't belong or whose inclusion will disrupt the status quo so much as to be beneficial for no one. One way to exclude blacks from the American dream was to physically separate them from whites and isolate them in communities where they could be more easily monitored, controlled, and, when necessary, punished. Separating them also made it easier to shape how they were viewed by the broader community.

> [T]he racialization of Blacks is literally mapped onto geographic locations as the urban ghetto replaced earlier systems of racial domination (slavery and Jim Crow) designed to suppress and control Black populations. Through individual, collective, and government action, White America constructed the ghetto. By segregating Blacks from Whites, they concentrated poverty and created a self-supported spiral of decline in urban Black neighborhoods. The ghetto—which has become an endemic intersection of race and class in the USA—has also become an important tool for isolating the byproducts of racial oppression—crime, violence, drugs, poverty, and despair. Today, these byproducts are often equated with Blackness and so African Americans are targeted by the police and the broader criminal justice system. The penal system is thus a crucial part of a uniquely American system of racial and social stratification. Like slavery and Jim Crow, both the ghetto and the criminal justice system are important "race-making" institutions, by marking those they confine as spoiled or debased and outside of mainstream or decent American society. Therefore, we can see the structural inequalities experienced by Blacks is firmly rooted in the nation's history, as both a product of, and integral to, their ongoing racialization. (Owusu-Bempah 2016, 26–27)

This cycle of criminalizing black existence reproduces itself without much question or concern from politicians and law makers. Once an African American, or a segment of an African American community, is deemed to be less than or prone to criminal behavior by a politician, law enforcement official, or conservative-news talking head, it usually doesn't take very long for other segments of society to believe and reinforce this belief. My belief in this idea is not based on any political leaning that I hold. It is based on data and experience.

To point out inequities in how a group of people is treated doesn't make a person more or less conservative or liberal. Standing against how African Americans are often mistreated through the criminal justice system doesn't mean a person wants to destroy that system. It means they recognize a problem that needs to be addressed in order for a group of people to be treated fairly.

One of the reasons I'm writing this book is to try to help the relationships between blacks and law enforcement before something else goes wrong. Those who experience the types of inequities I previously outlined will stand for it for only so long before they respond negatively to those whom they believe are mistreating them. This is what occurred in Ferguson, Missouri, after the killing of Michael Brown. The way the residents in Ferguson responded to Mr. Brown's death had as much to do with the unjust laws that had been enacted by that city's government to generate income on the backs of residents as it did with him being killed and left in the street like a common animal. That city's government created and used local laws as a way to make money primarily off the backs of black residents and visitors and to punish those same people when they weren't able, or willing, to get in line and do as they were told. Ferguson serves as a small example of how laws have been created and used throughout our nation's history to control and position certain populations.

HOW DOES THE RULE OF LAW SHAPE
THE STORYTELLING PROCESS?

Although media portrayals don't show this, the average American has no experience with the most severe and egregious crimes possible: felonies. Most crimes committed fall under the categories of municipal charges (like those utilized in Ferguson, Missouri) and misdemeanor infractions. These infractions serve the needs of those who seek to keep minority cultures separate from the dominant culture.

Misdemeanors constitute the bulk of the U.S. criminal justice apparatus, and they powerfully shape its institutional character and socioeconomic influence. Encompassing the vast majority of arrests and criminal cases—80 percent in the United States—petty offense enforcement is the mechanism through which the criminal system exerts its widest and, in many ways, deepest forms of social penetration and control. Reaching the most common behaviors and casual encounters, misdemeanor criminal enforcement empowers the state to touch, mark, burden, punish, and supervise millions of people, many of whom have not engaged in particularly culpable or harmful conduct. Because the petty offense process is largely informal and lacking in due process, it is relatively easy for the state to exert these forms of power and control, particularly over socially disadvantaged individuals and groups who lack legal and political protections. (Natapoff 2016, 1)

Misdemeanor violations have a long history of being used to either control certain populations or extract money from them. That money is then used to benefit those in power. This is what happened in Ferguson, Missouri. Political officials needed to find new sources of income to help fund the city's coffers, so they decided to do it on the backs of citizens through petty offenses and the overpolicing of groups of people: African Americans. This practice was not unique to Ferguson. It has been used throughout our nation's history.

We can see this process in the laws and practices that were created to re-enslave blacks after the Civil War. For example, as the Reconstruction experiment was being implemented in southern states, vagrancy laws were established and used to round up black males and divert them for forced labor, whether on a plantation or at a corporate headquarters. Scores of African Americans were charged with misdemeanor statutes, forced into hard labor—sometimes on plantations they had been freed from—and made to once again serve those who had previously owned them or their relatives.

Even though some of those laws are no longer in use in the same way, new ones have been developed and used to bring about the same results, just under a different legal title. If one thing has stayed consistent throughout our nation's history, it's the desire to control the movement of African Americans or people who have been deemed the least desirable. This is true in how loitering and trespassing statutes are enforced. As an officer, I was taught that these were some of the easiest violations to write and have prosecuted, and I witnessed people who had been deemed disrespectful by another officer locked up. This type of misdemeanor violation was used as a tool to control people on regular basis.

Although misdemeanors don't generate as much of an emotional response from law enforcement as do felonies, they still serve the purpose of being able to ensnare unsuspecting people into an all-encompassing web of legal fees and often fuzzy legal expectations. "Misdemeanors make up the vast majority of the American criminal system. Comprising approximately 80 percent of all arrests and 80 percent of state dockets, the petty offense process defines the criminal experience for most Americans, determining how the bulk of U.S. criminal convictions will be conferred and on whom" (Natapoff 2016, 3).

The misdemeanor system used by law enforcement and the courts serves to ensure that almost anything can be transformed into a crime that carries consequences that can appear to be as severe as felonies.

Structurally speaking, the misdemeanor system fulfills the core, complex governmental function of responding to and regulating low-level antisocial conduct. And like any largescale social institution, the system is not monolithic. Misdemeanor offenses include a wide variety of crimes, including drug possession, simple assault, driving on suspended license, petty theft, loitering, trespassing, and disorderly conduct. Some minor offenses aim at conduct that is harmful or culpable in the classic criminal sense—domestic violence, for example, or driving under the influence—making such misdemeanors look very much like small-scale felonies. At the federal level, misdemeanors typically receive due process comparable to felonies: counsel is routinely appointed, and hearings are held. (Natapoff 2016, 3–4)

The system of misdemeanor criminality is integral to the story that has been told because it allows law enforcement to consistently identify and arrest the types of people who benefit the continuing narrative that has been shaped. "The vast majority of misdemeanors criminalize common, low-level behaviors that involve small harms, or sometimes no harm at all, that are routinely engaged in by large numbers of people. It is this dynamic that generates the greatest societal challenges" (Natapoff 2016, 4).

There are consistent crimes that minority cultures are targeted for by law enforcement. Understanding three of these crimes in particular can help us to acknowledge the game that is played at the expense of many minority cultures.

There are at least three paradigmatic categories of common minor offenses in the United States: (1) driving on a suspended license, (2) marijuana possession, and (3) urban order crimes such as loitering, trespassing, disorderly conduct, and resisting arrest—what might be thought of as modern Blackstonian-type police offenses. Driving on a suspended license, for example, constitutes up to a third of many local dockets. It is an offense that, in effect, criminalizes poverty. It typically occurs when low-income individuals accrue traffic tickets they cannot afford to pay, leading to the suspension of their licenses. Millions of people lose their jobs and are plunged deeper into poverty when they lose their licenses as a result of this dynamic. Through offenses such as these, the misdemeanor process functionally singles out the poor and marks them with criminal convictions, which in turn exacerbate their underlying poverty. (Natapoff 2016, 4)

At a minimum, the misdemeanor system makes it possible for law enforcement to be strategic as it relates to where laws are enforced, who is forced to follow them, and who doesn't have to deal with communities that may bring with them certain behaviors or expectations. "In the United States in particular, petty offenses have a strong racial function. Police use loitering, trespassing, and disorderly conduct arrests to establish their authority over young black men, particularly in high crime communities, and to confer criminal records on low-income populations of color" (Natapoff 2016, 5).

The misdemeanor system also makes it possible for an ordinary person to become the target of police arrest quotas and the victim of a legal process that doesn't have the time or the inclination to see them as more than a number or another statistic in the story that has been told about the communities they come from. Municipal prosecutors, like those I interacted with when I was an officer, are typically managing a heavy case load. My experience was that if I built a positive working relationship with one of them, I could tell them which criminal cases I was presenting to them should be charged and which ones should be dismissed.

The system also makes it possible for entire groups of people who look a certain way or live in a particular type of community to be rounded up into nets of racial profiling with little hope of receiving due process. In the long run, if law enforcement wants to make a point to a certain community or group that the police are in control and they will force obedience or compliance on anyone they choose, the system, in effect, becomes a tool for law enforcement to ensure this is done.

At its core, misdemeanor laws and the process of enforcing them serve as one of the best tools available to those who want the story of criminality to have a black face. The system is widespread and can, on the one hand, be framed as a color-blind system, while on the other hand it can be used to target individuals or communities either one time or many. Since most whites don't have the misfortune of participating in the system, they don't understand how it can be bent for certain purposes. It is more likely that they believe justice is blind and evenly distributed.

One of the good things that occurs after incidents like Ferguson is that, over time, there is usually an increasing awareness of the inequities that emanate from the system of misdemeanor crime, and people begin to think about the implications and how to address the system so that it begins to function in a more just and equitable way. It becomes hard to ignore data and stories told by people who don't live in the same geographic areas but have almost identical experiences with law enforcement and the criminal justice system.

Although I have spent considerable time explaining the ins and outs of why the story of criminality is told, how it is told, and who tells it, you may be wondering whether anyone from the communities that are least likely to be affected by the laws and policies enacted to manage criminality in America care about what happens to people who probably would become criminals, regardless of how true or untrue any overblown conspiracy theory may be.

Judgments about the general fairness of the justice system are, to a great degree, experientially determined; quite commonly individuals will think about their own experiences, and those of their neighbors, as they evaluate the system as a whole. In contrast, at least for Whites, stereotypes of African Americans figure prominently into assessments of whether the justice system treats Blacks fairly. (Peffley and Hurwitz 2010, 111)

If a white person doesn't have any personal experiences with blacks that refute the stories that are told about them through the media, it will be hard for whites to mentally combat the images that are regularly presented to them about black criminality. Statistically and anecdotally, people are more likely to see images of blacks participating in some type of criminal enterprise than anything else. This image persists even though our nation has experienced the election of our first black president. When we watch the evening news or our favorite journalistic programs, we are more likely to see news stories that frame crime through an African American lens.

If a white person doesn't have any personal experiences with law enforcement that are similar to minorities, they are even less likely to have sympathy when minorities seek redress from police control or brutality. All of this leads to the reality that when blacks find themselves in majority-white settings or neighborhoods, whether on purpose or by accident, they are more than likely going to be viewed through the dual lenses of fear and suspicion: fear from what they may be capable of committing and suspicion of how long before that black person does something that fits the general stereotypes surrounding his existence.

When whites interact with blacks as part of the process to understand whether blacks really are as criminal as they are portrayed, the attitude held by the white person may be driven as much by paternalism that sees the majority of black life stemming from circumstances that forever destine black existence, neighborhoods, and communities to second-class status. This paternalistic attitude may have begun with law enforcement and media, but it has been securely ingrained in the minds and attitudes of the average everyday white person.

> Of course, the mistaken identification of individuals as potentially violent or dangerous is a phenomenon that is not isolated to law-enforcement circumstances. In contrast, this sort of situation is manifest in a variety of settings, including store clerks who keep a particularly keen eye on African American male customers who are targeted as potential shoplifters, and white women who clutch their pocketbooks more closely when in the presence of black men. (Oliver 2003, 3)

A CLOSER LOOK AT HOW POLICE PARTICIPATE IN THE STORYTELLING PROCESS

Law enforcement officials participate in the storytelling process based on what they see as the primary function of their position. That is the main question that they have to answer every day. Is their primary function to respond to citizen needs and complaints, or is it to find bad guys to bust and to grow their arrest statistics? Is it to answer radio calls, or is it to go out and look for high-profile drug felonies and misdemeanors? Way and present this question through a slightly different lens.

> What role should the police serve in a democratic society? Should police departments work to reduce crime and catch lawbreakers, or should their focus primarily be on responding to citizen calls for service or assistance? Of course, these strategies are not mutually exclusive, but one relies on police officers to ferret out crime and the other requires residents to report problems including crimes. (Way and Patten 2013, 1)

There is a historical disconnect between how police officers see their jobs versus how citizens view them. In general, officers are encouraged to do the things that will make them look good to their immediate line commander, the sergeant, which will in turn make their sergeant look better to the lieutenant, and the lieutenant to the captain, and on and on up the police department food chain. Officers typically aren't promoted or transferred to more desired assignments unless they have proven their worth as an officer. The typical way to prove your worth is to amass a significant number of arrests, not help citizens find answers to their ongoing social and family problems. Citizens, on the other hand, typically think officers are present in order to help them with a problem they are experiencing at the time, whether they have experienced or witnessed a violent crime, an accident, or an inconvenience. Citizens' agendas for officers can regularly conflict with what an officer wants to do or has been instructed to do by a superior commander.

On any given day that an officer patrols the streets of a municipality, there is always the chance that a work shift will be busy beyond any stretch of the imagination. But most days are not spent running from call to call for service. Instead, they are spent trying to figure out how to balance a manageable amount of radio calls with a personal desire to do things that will help officers build their street credibility among other officers.

There are also seasons that the number of radio calls an officer is asked to respond to goes down significantly. For example, when I was an officer, I knew that during the cold winter months of December through February, my daily load of calls would drop drastically because the combination of cold weather and shorter days forced people to stay indoors and live more sedentary lives, which led to fewer calls for service. During those seasons, officers would line up their patrol cars in rows and sleep for much of their shift.

Depending on the level of busyness on any given day, officers spend considerable time and discretion pursuing actions that they deem are in the best interest of their career, not the safety of a community. Officers who want to concentrate on increasing their drug arrest portfolio can make that their focus. Those who want to focus on traffic enforcement can choose to do that. As long as it's something that results in quantifiable arrests or citations, a commanding officer is likely going to be okay with what an officer chooses to focus on.

One of the challenges that comes with this practice is that helping citizens gain access to needed resources or how to manage life's emergencies in a way that is respectful and compassionate is typically not a high priority for the average street cop because they don't get rewarded for helping citizens by the system they serve in. For most police departments, officers are rewarded for achieving a certain number of arrests, for writing a certain number of parking tickets, or for how much legal pain they are able to inflict upon citizens, whether that pain is intentional or unintentional.

When officers have the time to start a self-initiated investigation, it likely revolves around trying to make a high-profile misdemeanor or felony arrest, because those are the kinds of arrests that people remember when they are considering who to make detective or to give a choice patrol assignment. Unfortunately, when officers want to make these kinds of arrests, they will look to make them in communities filled with poor or minorities. Primarily because, although whites and blacks utilize illegal drugs at the same level, it is considered easier to arrest and successfully prosecute poor people and minorities partly due to the fact that, in all likelihood, they will not have the monetary resources necessary to successfully fight a criminal charge or to acquire adequate legal counsel.

> There are institutional and organizational structures and incentives within both the police department and the criminal justice process that induce officers to patrol the poor, especially those from racial and ethnic minorities, to a greater degree; and the institutional goal to produce citations and arrests leads officers to proactively patrol. Note that both of these arguments are addressing the effects of institutional incentives and organizational structures. (Way and Patten 2013, 3–4)

Understanding what the system of policing requires of officers can hopefully lead to the common citizen having a better understanding of the position officers are typically placed in by the departments that employ them. As much as we may wish it were true, an officer's first job isn't to help citizens. It's to make the system they work in happy. You make the system happy by being productive. Being productive may require officers to do things they wouldn't typically do in their ordinary lives, but in order to stay in the system and/or move up within the system, they have to play by the rules the system sets. It's not as simple as we hope it is. Most police systems are complicated by the need to make sure that they remain in existence. The primary way to maintain existence is for the system to produce data that shows the system is doing something tangible. This data is easiest to see and reconcile through the number of arrests made or citations written, which in turn leads to revenue for the local tax base or grants from federal departments.

From my experience as an officer, if a city or municipality has an urban or poorer community, the system of policing will encourage, and in some cases require, officers to patrol specific neighborhoods in tougher ways than they do others in order to increase arrest and citation statistics. One reason is because crime does occur in these areas.

> We find here that proactive work, or hunting, by officers is almost exclusively done within economically poor neighborhoods—where racial minorities are more likely to be found. The result is racial minorities are subject to a greater level of surveillance than their White counterparts. (Way and Patten 2013, 5)

Another reason is the belief that those neighborhoods have fewer physical and legal resources at their disposal, and most prosecutors and juries will believe a police officer over people from poor or black neighborhoods. This is not necessarily true for more affluent neighborhoods. Residents in more affluent communities typically have adequate resources and connections to legal resources. This can cause officers to think twice about how they treat members of communities that have access to resources.

In poorer urban communities, officers have the opportunity to initiate practices they wouldn't be able to institute in more affluent neighborhoods without fear of too much legal reprisal or pushback from the higher-ups within their department because the system believes this is the way things should be. Officers who patrol differing communities in differing ways are usually rewarded for their efforts, not punished. "They view these roles as the main part of their job, if not the only part of their job, and their administrations either support this effort or are indifferent to it" (Way and Patten 2013, 6).

THE STORY THAT STYLES OF POLICING TELL ABOUT AN OFFICER'S PRIORITIES

Although multiple types of personalities choose to participate in the world of law enforcement, Way and Patten have identified four specific styles of policing that are typically practiced by officers. There are enforcers, hunters, slugs, and community builders. Officers make a conscious decision every day about which category they will fit in. The policing style they choose dictates how they will interact with citizens and other officers.

STYLES OF POLICING

The following are a list of typical styles employed by officers and corresponding descriptions of how those styles are implemented when interacting with citizens.

- Enforcers believe their job is to keep the streets safe, but there are a variety of ways to achieve that goal, and officers can focus on different offenses in order to feel as if they are fighting crime. There is also a distinction between active and passive officers. Active officers are those who initiate more contacts with citizens, assert control, and make more arrests.

- Hunters were those officers who saw proactive policing as a positive aspect of their job and would devote time during a shift to make sure they did proactive work. Officers who exhibited a hunting policing style were actively looking for lawbreakers rather than waiting for a community member to identify criminal activity. During a shift, they were more likely to make resident contacts with the sole purpose of exposing criminal activity. Hunters indicated they sought felony arrests and pursued criminals because those activities were fun and exciting.

- The term *slug* is one used by officers themselves to describe their peers who did very little hunting. Slugs, also defined as "station queens," are officers whose policing style involves little proactive work while staying within the parameters of institutional influences and administrative expectations. Some slugs are predisposed to avoid not only proactive work but also as much work in general as possible. Slugs had fewer citations, arrests, and resident contacts. They were also not as valued as those who were considered hunters, because slugs did not personify the image of a crime fighter. Hunters would often refer to officers with this policing style as "lazy."

- Community builders displayed behavior that was consistent with community policing approaches. (Way and Patten 2013, 32–33)

Hopefully the reader can see that the type of officer you want to be influences how you will view and respond to citizens as you interact with them on a regular basis. Your policing style will determine whether you see citizens as a means, an end, or means to an end. Will you serve the needs of citizens, or do they serve your professional needs for promotion or garnering overtime?

The reader should be able to recognize some of the challenges that are inherent in most of these policing styles. Hunters are less likely to view calls for service as a legitimate use of their time. Hunters are also more likely to employ harsher measures to locate crime. They are also more likely to view inhabitants in a community they deem "less than" as potential suspects. In addition, they are more likely to follow a hunch or their "gut" when looking for potential criminal actions. The problem with this practice is hunches and guts are often influenced by preconceived ideas about certain groups of people. One of the challenges I remember as an officer was that these types of attitudes and actions tended to be the ones that were usually rewarded with promotions and choice patrol or undercover assignments.

IS ONE STYLE OF POLICING BETTER OR WORSE THAN ANOTHER?

The answer to that question depends on what side of the question you stand. If you are an officer who believes that aggression is not only needed but expected, to show your co-workers and supervisors that you can be trusted to pull your weight in arrests, citations, and the other statistical categories your department has deemed most important, being a hunter is the way to go. But if you hope to learn who community members are, understand their life circumstances and why they are interacting with law enforcement, and meet their needs on their terms, you may seek to be a community builder. If you hope to find a healthy balance between those two, you may seek to be an enforcer with a sympathetic heart and ear.

Obviously, much of this will be affected by the priorities of an officer's day-to-day frontline supervisor. Do they advocate proactive policing, sometimes called order maintenance policing, or do they want you to primarily answer radio calls? Is the goal of policing building stats or is it building better relationships with community members? The choice doesn't have to be one or the other, but that is typically how officers see it. You either want to actively seek out crime, or you want to wait until you have to work.

As previously identified, proactive policing is the process of officers actively and intentionally seeking to identify crime as it is occurring or before it occurs. Some call it order maintenance policing or broken windows policing. The idea is that in identifying and punishing minor offenses, people will be deterred from committing greater offenses or allowing them to be committed. As you can imagine, this type of policing leads to several challenges for citizens living in particular types of communities.

> The evidence shows that when officers are expected to make a high number of citizen contacts, the discretionary decisions they make regarding who they should contact is influenced by society's views of who is criminal and who is not. Officers are shaped, as we all are, by the norms, cultural practices, and assumptions that have shaped the United States. There is a historical legacy of racism in the United States, and time has not eliminated this racial strife. The choices police officers make regarding whether they will hunt, to what

degree they will hunt, and what particular crimes they will hunt, largely influence how officers interact with the poorer members of a community. (Way
and Patten 2013, 15)

Inevitably, this style of policing is not practiced across all communities. It
is utilized primarily in neighborhoods and communities that law enforcement deems to be disorderly and deserves to be controlled. Within this
philosophy, the potential relationships that could be built between law
enforcement and the citizenry are not given the chance to be built or blos-
som. The opposite typically occurs to the detriment of all involved. Most
of these communities are not looking for more crime fighters, but instead
are looking for partners who will work with them to identify problem areas
and problem people, and together develop a plan that will make their communities safer without them feeling like they are being occupied or controlled by an uncaring, opportunistic occupying force.

3

The Aftereffects of the Story

"[A]t the same time and in the same society [the police institution] may be both the agent of the people it polices and of the dominant class controlling these same people" (Robinson and Scaglion 1987, 109).

As this book begins to draw near to its conclusion, I want to identify some of the aftereffects of the story of policing that's being told and whom it affects. I identify these aftereffects knowing that citizens have a certain view of what police should do that doesn't always line up with the realities of policing. In general, citizens expect that officers and departments will be primarily concerned with responding to calls for service, participating in active community patrols with the express intent of preemptively identifying and dealing with potential criminal behavior, and spending time with citizens through various initiatives, such as community-based meetings, in order for both groups to learn more about each other and determine best steps for them to work together for the common good.

The views that citizens hold toward police are subject to change over time based on whether officers and departments are willing to actively engage with citizens to proactively identify challenges and opportunities for partnership, as well as an officer's willingness to be in relationship with citizens before something has gone wrong or whether a high-profile situation has occurred. With that in mind, I identify the following as concerns officers and departments should regularly be aware of as they seek to figure out ways to better be in relationship with the communities they patrol.

First, when police don't patrol differing communities in equitable ways, the reputation of law enforcement is damaged. Citizens may not believe that police have anyone's best interests at heart other than their own. Relationships that could benefit both law enforcement and citizens never receive an opportunity to be discussed and/or nurtured. Instead, minorities push back against law enforcement, typically to their own demise.

I say that it is to their own demise because minorities usually don't come out on the winning side when they take law enforcement head on and request or demand changes in how they are patrolled. History is replete with instances of minority groups banding together to challenge the system that is law enforcement only to become victims to law enforcement in new, unimagined ways. The system that is policing isn't first concerned about the citizens it patrols. It is first concerned about gaining obedience and compliance from those people in the hopes of that obedience and compliance making an officer's job easier.

Police don't welcome public dissent from citizens. They want unquestioned respect and obedience. This is verified by the plethora of videos chronicling the interaction between officers and people from minority communities that are available on YouTube. Those videos regularly show police insistence on immediate compliance from minority citizens with swift and harsh penalties for not obeying. Typical public responses to these types of videos by white viewers is that black citizens should have done what they were told.

Second, if we don't see minorities, especially black and brown people, as equal to whites, then they can be treated in less humane ways when they interact with law enforcement and the criminal justice system. If minorities aren't fully human, their neighborhoods and communities can be patrolled in ways that resemble military occupation. Resources don't have to be allocated to them, since they will likely waste them and not appreciate them. And police become heroes because they deal with the people that we don't want to deal with and make our lives and communities safer by not allowing minorities to interact or engage with us in certain ways.

As I have emphasized in other chapters, this was not done haphazardly. This process served to shape a larger agenda of determining who was welcome where in America and who could do what while here.

The idea of black criminality was crucial to the making of modern urban America. In nearly every sphere of life it impacted how people defined fundamental differences between native whites, immigrants, and blacks. It also impacted, by comparison, how people evaluated black people's presence—the Negro Problem, as it had once been called—in the urban North. In education, in housing, in jobs, in leisure and recreation, the idea shaped the "public transcript" of the modern urban world. Moreover, the various ways in which writers and reformers imagined black people as inferior to and fundamentally different from native whites and immigrants in the early twentieth century had a direct impact on the allocation of social resources for preventing crime in all communities, with the smallest amount flowing to black communities. (Muhammad 2010, 272–273)

This process also served to help redefine what it meant to be an American. Previously, immigrants, like the Irish, were not considered American. Because of their criminal tendencies, white Americans shunned the Irish. But as the desire to criminalize black conduct increased, the desire to criminalize Irish behavior decreased. A new villain had been identified, which eventually led to a reconsideration of the place of Irish people within America. In the end, even with their inherent foreignness, the Irish and other groups of people were welcomed in our nation because they weren't black.

> Thoughtful, well-funded crime prevention and politically accountable crime fighting secured immigrants' whiteness, in contrast to the experiences of blacks, who were often brutalized or left unprotected and were repeatedly told to conquer their own crime before others would help them. The destructive consequences of the black crime discourse went beyond limited reform efforts in black communities; it also limited the application of pioneering sociological concepts to record and interpret the black experience. (Muhammad 2010, 273)

This process even affects how educational systems are funded on local and state levels, which affect how and what children from minority communities learn and understand is valuable. "[O]n the state and local level crime control expenditures are given priority over educational expenditures" (Chambliss 2018, 133). Apparently, it makes more sense to the powers that be to devote substantial resources to housing and controlling people after a crime has been committed than to interact with them and help them understand the power of positive life choices and how that can benefit everyone.

If we don't care very much about minorities, see them primarily as dehumanized, and view them as merely a means to an end to ensure that police departments are funded in more extensive ways, police can patrol minority neighborhoods with ever-increasing levels of violence against citizens without much concern for reprisal from the powers that be. We don't question why armored police vehicles are used in primarily minority communities and not in predominantly white ones. We get used to seeing tear gas, stun guns, and other lethal-force tools used when groups of African Americans gather to protest something, regardless of the size of the group, because we believe that any size group of blacks can become disruptive and dangerous at any given time, but we don't see the same police response when whites gather together, even openly brandishing firearms, because we recognize their right to gather and bear arms any time they choose without many legal repercussions.

If minorities are less than human, police can create compelling arguments about the need to over-enforce laws strategically in minority communities to produce more compelling law enforcement results (arrest and citation statistics), which justify the need to increase budgets. It is also used to justify plans for increased manpower, which in turn continues the process of over-patrolling those communities. The fallout for this type of tactic is typically minimal. "The use of violence by the police is seen as necessary and is rewarded formally and informally. Even when citizen complaints succeed in exposing violence and a victim is awarded large sums of money by the courts, the officers responsible are not held accountable" (Chambliss 2018, 122).

Third in this never-ending story of policing, based on their personal experiences with police, whites are more likely to worship police and to believe their reasoning for patrolling minority communities as they do and less likely to try to hold them accountable for their actions. On the opposite side, due to how many black people's opinions about law enforcement have been shaped by bad legal policies and less-than-kind policing tactics in their lives, blacks typically distrust police and the system they serve.

> In accounting for the over-representation of Blacks in police and other justice statistics, and in attempting to uncover racial bias, we have also largely ignored what Ward describes as "slow violence," the structural violence of deprivation that serves to establish economic inequalities and maintain relations of racial domination and subordination. These include physical violence, property destruction, and dispossession over the past two centuries that continue to foster generational poverty, poor work prospects, neighborhood change, racial resentment, and distrust of police. (Owusu-Bempah 2016, 25)

Fourth, people are affected negatively, generations are scarred, and chasms grow between law enforcement and communities, and we don't seem to be any closer to developing a system of law enforcement that treats all people as innocent until proven guilty.

"Dire consequences follow from these institutionalized patterns of creating myths about crime, defining lower-class minorities as inherently criminal, and selectively enforcing criminal laws. The minorities who experience the sting of the law are alienated from society and see the law not as a source of protection but as a mechanism of oppression" (Chambliss 2018, 134).

Fifth, the process of policing that is currently in practice misses out on shedding light on other equally deserving victims and criminals because its focus is primarily on certain drug arrests that occur for the most part in minority communities. The field of criminality has previously identified multiple other areas that would benefit from one-tenth the scrutiny that is given to drug crimes and the crimes of minorities. Instead, law enforcement and legal personnel focus primarily on one group and fail to see how other types of crimes affect our nation in even greater ways and cover more ground as they trickle down through our nation. "(Traditional narcotics strategy), though it may end with the chief of police and the district attorney holding a press conference in front of a table filled with seized drug product, does not address long-term solutions or root causes through real, sustained problem-solving" (Mentel 2012, 12).

In the end, I don't think that we, meaning our nation—especially those who are most capable of changing the types of disconnections that I have tried to outline through this book—want to do the hard, long, and painful work of dealing with our legacy of law enforcement that began as ways to keep minority cultures separated from whites and continues this process now. Instead, we would rather deal with peripheral discussions surrounding the bigger problem. That's what I think has been occurring when athletes and entertainers try to bring light to the common experience shared by most blacks.

We see this practice in the nationwide conversations revolving around Colin Kaepernick and his decisions to first sit and then kneel during the national anthem. He did this to try to bring light to the subject of police brutality toward blacks. Instead of serving as a model for what these types of conversations can look like, this discussion continues to serve as a symbol of what's wrong with how our nation discusses race and policing and how certain minority groups are viewed and treated, especially when they interact with law enforcement.

Instead of dealing with the issue that Mr. Kaepernick has attempted to bring to light, athletes and other public figures have spent their time debating whether or not his decline from being a starting quarterback to a second-string quarterback to a former quarterback qualifies him to make public statements about how police treat black people. People on the police side of the discussion have failed to address the questions he raised and instead try to focus conversations on whether he's been converted to radical Islam by his Muslim girlfriend or whether his perceived lack of patriotism disqualifies him from having a legitimate opinion about anything of note.

These peripheral conversations serve only to divert our attention away from Mr. Kaepernick's original point of discussion: the experiences that black and brown people have when they come into contact with police. The tactics used to try to discredit Mr. Kaepernick and deflect attention from the issue that he's trying to address have been outlined in the book *48 Laws of Power*, written by Robert Greene.

In *48 Laws of Power*, Mr. Greene outlines three tactics that clearly apply to how Mr. Kaepernick has been viewed and presented through mainstream media. Law 31 says, "Control the options—get others to play with the cards you deal. The best deceptions are the ones that seem to give the other person a choice: Your victims feel they are in control but are actually your puppets. Give people options that come out in your favor whichever one they choose. Force them to make choices between the lesser of two evils, both of which serve your purpose. Put them on the horns of a dilemma: They are gored wherever they turn" (Greene 2000, 254).

The false dilemma of the current conversation about race and policing is that you either have to be for police or against them. There is no middle ground. Once you take a stand, in Kaepernick's case a knee, against police brutality, you are immediately branded as someone who hates all police and supports all criminals. Neither of these is actually true. We are told that there is no middle ground, but there is, and it's up to discerning citizens to make sure that middle ground isn't lost.

Law 37 states, "Create compelling spectacles. Striking imagery and grand symbolic gestures create the aura of power—everyone responds to them. Stage spectacles for those around you, then full of arresting visuals and radiant symbols that heighten your presence. Dazzled by appearances, no one will notice what you are really doing" (Greene 2000, 309).

What better spectacle than the celebrations that occur when the U.S. flag is raised before a sporting event? By requiring people to take part in the celebration of the flag as a public symbol of their patriotism, the spectacle is on the gesture and not remembering or questioning the principles and practices that helped to make America the great nation that it is. Practices such as believing in, and adhering to, a philosophy of Manifest Destiny in order to justify exerting personal and social power and authority over those who were militarily weaker and less sophisticated.

Law 42 states, "Strike the shepherd and the sheep will scatter. Trouble can often be traced to a single strong individual—the stirrer, the arrogant underling, the poisoned of goodwill. If you allow such people room to operate, others will succumb to their influence. Do not wait for the troubles they cause to multiply, do not try to negotiate with them—they are irredeemable. Neutralize their influence by isolating or banishing them. Strike at the source of the trouble and the sheep will scatter" (Greene 2000, 358).

The act of silencing the lead troublemaker has been the primary practice of those who oppose equal rights. The thought is that if you can silence their voice, you can silence their influence. Or if you inflict enough pain on that person, those who follow them will fear experiencing the same thing and cease to follow them. The irony of how Mr. Kaepernick has been treated is that it has actually led to more people following his lead and imitating him.

Mr. Greene's laws can be summarized through the words distract, divide, and conquer. *Distract* from the actual subject that was originally brought up by not addressing it, and instead bring attention to something totally unrelated. *Divide* by making the new issue that you have brought up the thing to be focused on and villainize anyone who tries to bring the conversation back to its original point of focus. *Conquer* those who tried to bring attention to the original problem by making them out to be the bad guy for bringing the subject up in the first place.

As a former police officer, I know that Mr. Greene's laws are used by police departments when they want to silence someone who makes them look bad. Instead of dealing with the problem of police abuse and misconduct head on, many people attempt to draw our attention away from its reality and focus on peripheral things, like the national anthem. Instead of spending so much time questioning Mr. Kaepernick's patriotism, we should be working on solutions that help police officers not immediately judge black males as being dangerous or immediately assume that they are "bad dudes" who are "on something," as the helicopter pilot exclaimed about Mr. Crutcher. In focusing on legitimate solutions, we will hopefully be able to save more lives. What's more patriotic than that?

4

How Can the Story End Better?

"Proactive relationship building affords a police department, not a 'free pass,' but ... 'a moment of pause,' the period just after a high-profile, emotionally charged incident when the chief has time to 'pick up the phone and call community leaders to the table'" (Mentel 2012, 18).

I don't want this book to only be about what's wrong with policing. I want it to also express a certain level of hope that I have for the future of policing and how it interacts with people in the real world. I am a former officer, and I realize that police don't necessarily want to be viewed as the enemy of communities. For the most part, they don't want to be seen as an occupying force that only seeks to harm people. They want to be seen as professionals who take their job seriously. They want to be trusted by the communities they serve.

I remember what it felt like to be a teenage boy who was stopped by police while walking out of my front yard and being told that I looked like someone the officer had previously arrested and even if I wasn't that person, I looked like I was up to no good. I remember being pulled over by police while driving because I didn't look like I belonged in a particular neighborhood, even though I was working as a construction laborer in that neighborhood. I know what it feels like to be pulled over because I was driving the speed limit and have the officer tell me that only people who were committing crimes drove the speed limit.

I also remember what it was like to strap on a bulletproof vest, gun belt, and badge every day and carry the physical and metaphorical weight that the uniform brought. I remember what it was like to respond to call after call after call. To go to a home every week and try to help people deal with problems that had nothing to do with me and thinking, "Can't you people get your lives together? It's not my job to fix your family." To feel the pain of people who didn't feel like they had much to hope or live for. To feel the pressure when a commanding officer told me that it wasn't my job to try to fix people. Instead, my job was to answer calls and, when necessary, make as many arrests as I could so people would know that jail was where they would end up if they didn't get their act together.

Police aren't perfect. Police departments aren't perfect. The people and neighborhoods they patrol aren't perfect. The relationships they have with each other aren't perfect. But we exist together. That mutual existence is often fraught with misunderstandings, preconceived ideas and attitudes, and bad blood. But we can do better by each other if we are willing to take responsibility for our individual actions and try to live together in more intentional ways. I know this may sound trite, but my faith and experience lead me to believe this.

One of the first steps in attaining better relationships is for citizens to acknowledge their part in facilitating the relationship that exists between citizens and law enforcement. As much as we may want to blame police for all the problems that exist in our relationship with them, they are not always at fault.

> To be clear . . . the police should not carry all blame for this complex dynamic; municipal policing, after all, was designed to be a safety mechanism for a community when informal social controls fail. The wide-ranging and systemic root causes for the structural inequalities existing in America's most troubled neighborhoods extend far beyond the reach and responsibility of law enforcement alone. Yet law enforcement often singlehandedly bears the burden of addressing the crime and violence issues that are symptomatic of these underlying problems. (Mentel 2012, 5)

Although officers are often viewed as heroes who have all the answers, or at least have the power and resources to make certain decisions, their job functions are often narrow and specific, even if citizens don't know, understand their functions, or like what police are supposed to do. During my time as an officer, I learned that my job wasn't first to help people or make life easier for citizens. My first job was to figure out how to convince people to stop calling 911 for help with things they should already know how to do or fix for themselves.

Priority one was to get people to stop bothering me and other officers with nonsense. Everything else fell in line after that. Yes, I may eventually help someone with something they needed or eventually stop something bad from recurring, but those were all secondary benefits. The first concern was figuring out how to convince people to handle their own problems, their own family members, their own relationships so they would stop calling the police.

We all know that it's not our job to cause more problems for people, but we also have to recognize that it's not law enforcement's job to fix every problem that a family or community faces. When and where it's in our power to make changes that benefit us and our communities, we should make concerted efforts to bring about change that enables and empowers us and others to do good among and for ourselves, regardless of police participation. As a part of the process of developing improved citizen and police relationships, citizens can take a greater level of leadership in developing initiatives to improve their own communities outside of calling the police every time something goes wrong. This can take the form of a neighborhood watch, regular community-led meetings, and community-wide strategic planning to address common issues and concerns. Mentel writes:

> An admission, such as "we have not been enforcing right and wrong within our own communities," can be enough to begin productive conversations with law enforcement, which already knows it cannot solve these problems alone. Such an admission also signals to police, who often feel accused of being unilaterally culpable for sustained levels of violence and mass incarceration, that the community is willing to concede its own past mistakes, move forward, and work collaboratively. (Mentel 2012, 19)

For a community and its members to recognize the part they can actively play in making their lives safer is not an admission that they have previously failed or done something wrong. It's simply acknowledging that as much as we may need police to help make communities safer, we have our own responsibilities to make sure that community-wide change begins with us.

I recognize that poor and minority neighborhoods don't necessarily want to have to depend on police to keep their neighborhoods safe. But due to how police have used their powers to punish not only individuals but entire neighborhoods, poor and minority communities don't believe they can trust law enforcement. They don't want their neighborhoods overrun with crime, but they don't necessarily trust police to help them without somehow punishing them as well. Because of this fear, they sometimes will not cooperate with police when they make efforts to address crime. This hesitance to cooperate is often seen as disingenuousness by officers.

> Most chiefs (and officers) think silence (by a community when a crime has occurred) is satisfaction. No, it is not. It's just silence. Too often, law enforcement mistakes this silence (the perceived lack of outrage, the absence of candlelight vigils and marches on city hall) for, at best, apathy for and, at

worst, complicity in the cycle of violence that continues to afflict poor, urban neighborhoods. (Mentel 2012, 8)

My second suggestion is for departments to take the time to listen to citizen complaints and actually recognize their validity. When we take time to have uncomfortable conversations, like the one I'm trying to have through this book, we are able to get to the heart of circumstances. Then we are able to better understand why citizens who claim to want better for their communities don't necessarily view cooperating with police as a viable option. Citizen silence or lack of cooperation with police doesn't mean they are complicit. It could mean they are afraid of repercussions from the criminal element in their community if they cooperate with law enforcement. It could mean that they are afraid that law enforcement may not really be concerned about them or their communities and instead see them as statistics to help them get promoted. Their silence and uncooperativeness are not signs of acquiescence, but signs that they don't believe they can trust a system that, in many ways, was built to keep them separated from people who don't like them, trust them, or see them as fully human and worthy of equal respect and treatment.

This isn't something rich and middle-class white neighborhoods usually have to deal with. When police respond to their communities, they typically do it with a high degree of respect for citizens. This isn't always true in African American communities. The opposite is often what occurs, regardless of whether the African American community is low income, middle class, or affluent. As an officer, I responded to calls in all types of communities in St. Louis. The white callers were overwhelmingly treated with respect and courtesy, while black callers were typically treated like they were wasting the officer's time by calling. Or black callers were punished for calling police in the first place. Officers regularly threatened black callers with arrest if they called 911 in the future, or the officer found a way to punish the caller before they left the scene.

For example, I once assisted a white officer who responded to a call at an African American home. The citizen didn't like the way the white officer was interacting with her, so she closed the front door in the officer's face. The officer responded by kicking the door in and arresting her for peace disturbance. I witnessed both white and black officers commit these types of acts against citizens. The reader may wonder why I never reported behavior like this to superior officers. Within the first three months of my employment, I learned to never cross another officer, because they would always find out and I would be the one who would be punished for speaking out against them.

This difference in attitudes toward black versus white callers can be present, regardless of whether the officer is black or white. It can also be true whether the community is primarily black and the police force and chief are white or the police force and chief are black. I learned this firsthand when I worked as a police officer for the city of St. Louis, an urban city with a substantial African American presence, under the leadership of multiple black police chiefs.

When I began patrolling the streets, our chief was black. After his retirement, the next chief was white. Following his retirement, the next chief, Dan Isom, was black. He was also the first chief in St. Louis history to have earned a PhD in criminology and criminal justice. After his retirement from policing, Dr. Isom became a full-time professor teaching criminology and criminal justice at a state university. The common thread between all three chiefs was that during all their tenures, St. Louis was ranked as one of the most dangerous cities in our nation. Having a black or white chief didn't improve community relations, and it most definitely didn't make a dent in homicide levels.

For a little under one year, I worked as a public affairs officer within a predominantly African American district that had a reputation for being financially disadvantaged and extremely violent. Part of my job was to facilitate monthly meetings between citizen groups and help them work toward solutions to the challenges facing their neighborhood, as well as hear their suggestions for how the police department could assist them. Citizens consistently advocated for the department to patrol their black neighborhoods the same as white communities, show the same level of respect to them when they sought assistance from police as when white citizens did, and for police to not assume that because the neighborhood was black that its inhabitants were inherently criminal.

Some of the pushback that officers provided against these citizen statements was that black citizens didn't want anything to change in their communities because they didn't cooperate with police in the ways that police wanted. Because of this lack of cooperation, police believed that most citizens were complicit in the negative things that were occurring in the community. This assumption by police is grossly incorrect. Anecdotal and statistical data shows that blacks are just as concerned about crime as whites. One of the primary differences in how they respond to crime that may be present in their communities is that they distrust law enforcement more than whites based on their personal experiences of how police treat them and over-police them.

Third, for citizens who want to actively participate in healing and rebuilding the lines of communication between citizens and officers, I offer the following list of suggestions:

- Every citizen who is concerned about how officers do their job should attend a local police department's citizen on patrol academy or citizens police academy.

- Citizens can volunteer to participate in, or seek to be elected to, their local police department's citizen review board.
- It would help everyone if citizens became familiar with the various city departments that serve the needs of people in their neighborhoods.
- This may sound nitpicky, but citizens have to teach their children and grandchildren how to properly interact with law enforcement.
  - We should teach our children that officers do have a certain level of authority at all times. When a policeman gives a person an appropriate legal command, that command should be followed, not challenged.
  - Hopefully the reader noticed that I said "appropriate legal command" and not "appropriate level of force." I do not advocate or defend officers who arrive on the scene and start out by busting heads and then asking questions. Officers who do not follow the legal and social parameters that are set for them should be held subject to punishment as any other citizen would.
- Community members should also teach their children to always keep their hands where an officer can see them.
  - If someone hides their hands, whether on purpose or accident, an officer will immediately think that they are reaching for something to cause them bodily harm. Unfortunately, this is the nature of the beast. Too many officers have been harmed when a person was able to reach into their pockets and retrieve a knife or gun.
- We all must acknowledge and deal with the fact that much of the crime and killings that are perpetrated on the black community are committed by black people, not police officers.
  - Yes, police officers have killed unarmed black people. This is never acceptable. Officers must be held accountable and justice must be found for victims of police abuse. But we must also recognize that it is easier for us to point out the sins and grievances of someone else before we acknowledge our own sins or the sins of our children. It is easier to point out a white officer who treated me poorly than to publicly criticize a young black child from my own neighborhood who regularly breaks into cars. (Carter 2015, 35–38)

Fourth, an equally important step in the process to bridge the gap between citizens and police is for law enforcement to acknowledge the role they have played in creating the tension and mistrust that exist. But what should their first step be in this process? I think it is for them to openly acknowledge the history of policing and its relationship to minority cultures and somehow express remorse. It is necessary for citizens to hear that police know that grave misdeeds have been committed in the past and that citizens have not always been respected, but law enforcement wants the relationship to change for the better. This should be done in tandem by departments that have historically negative histories. I know that this suggestion will be summarily dismissed by law enforcement because a person or department shouldn't have to apologize for what someone else did. I understand why police officials may feel this way but denying the verifiable history between citizens and police doesn't help anyone. "Whether or not law enforcement acknowledges this past role, both the police and the community are currently inheriting problems associated with it" (Mentel 2012, 3).

Another reason law enforcement may not want to apologize for past indiscretions is they may be concerned about potential lawsuits that lead to the possibility of having to compensate communities if they admit wrong doing. Yet another reason may be the fear of fostering the perception that they are giving some of their power away to citizens.

> [T]here is rarely any political benefit to officials in "owning" a police brutality problem. Instead, police often fear that losing control of the brutality issue will lead directly or indirectly to decreased police autonomy if the public's "second guessing" becomes institutionalized in more restrictive use-of-force policies or in more formal processes for civilian review of allegations of police misconduct. Consequently, police often see allegations of brutality as dangerous invitations to the public and political officials to circumscribe police authority and discretion. (Lawrence 2000, 23)

But if departments really want to build positive relationships with minority communities, those communities want—a better word may be need—to know that police are willing to acknowledge past actions, the pain those actions caused in those communities, and that they truly see minorities as fully human and that what they bring to the relationship is just as important as what an officer brings. A high-profile example of an officer apologizing for past events occurred in 2016. Terrence Cunningham, police chief of Wellesley, Massachusetts, offered an apology to communities of color. Chief Cunningham said the apology was necessary to "[Clear] a path that allows us to move beyond our history and identify common solutions to better protect our communities" (Craven 2016). Chief Cunningham continues:

> For our part, the first step in this process is for law enforcement . . . to acknowledge and apologize for the actions of the past and the role that our profession has played in society's historical mistreatment of communities of color. There have been times when law enforcement officers, because of the laws enacted by federal, state and local governments, have been the face of oppression for far too many of our fellow citizens. In the past, the laws adopted by our society have required police officers to perform many

unpalatable tasks, such as ensuring legalized discrimination or even denying the basic rights of citizenship to many of our fellow Americans. (Craven
2016)

As you can imagine, Chief Cunningham's words were met with broad support but also dissent. I believe that some type of apology or stated recogni-
tion of the past is a necessary first step in bridging the divide because of
the long-term effects of prior practices, discrimination, and tension. His
words were a welcome relief from political rhetoric that seems to want to
keep people divided instead of united. It was reminiscent of other well-
known words offered by leaders seeking to heal and unify people after
times of turmoil.

Not everyone wanted to hear the apology or believed it was necessary.
They may have been right. "Admittedly, an apology may not be appropriate
in every community and in all circumstances and entering into a frank discussion of race and policing does not necessarily require one" (Mentel
2012, 17). There may be other ways to mend fences or move more positively
into the future. Whether or not an apology is offered, law enforcement has
to figure out a way that lets citizens know their humanity is recognized and
that they are wanted at the table to develop new strategies for improving
communication between the two groups.

Another necessary step in the healing process is for departments to
actively instill a new creed for officers that changes the mind-set that citizens aren't an enemy that simply needs to be controlled. "Repairing relationships may start organizationally with the chief, but the legitimacy of the
department fundamentally depends on how police officers treat people on
the street" (Mentel 2012, 5). This may mean higher standards need to be
set for who can and can't become an officer.

A better way of saying this may be that departments have to take seriously their decisions on who they will hire. Officer Timothy Loehmann is
an example of what I mean. Officer Loehmann previously worked for an
Ohio department, but was fired after supervising officers determined that
he was unfit for the job. He was subsequently hired a short time later by
the Cleveland Police Department. Shortly after being given his first assignment for the Cleveland Department, he shot and killed Tamir Rice, a teen-
ager who was sitting in a park holding a toy gun. Loehmann was subsequently
fired in 2014 from the Cleveland department, not for killing Rice, but
because it was later revealed that he lied on his initial job application. In
October 2018, he was hired as an officer for another municipality.

I don't believe that it is wrong for a person to receive a second or third
chance to provide for themselves and their family, but if that person has
shown a tendency to be unfit for a job that requires a certain level of matu-
rity, tact, and truthfulness, which, based on his history, Loehmann doesn't

seem to consistently exhibit, that person shouldn't be given a second or third chance in that particular field. Despite the fact that it will likely lead to a public relations nightmare, it also puts civilians and that officer in a tenuous situation. The officer likely will feel that they have to defend their honor at every turn, and citizens will feel that the department cares more about protecting one of their own and not putting the most qualified officers on the street.

I'm not a practicing psychologist, and I'm not trying to psychoanalyze Loehmann, but one of the ways to combat this is to understand why someone wants to become an officer in the first place. In suggesting this, I'm not assuming that every officer wants to patrol the streets because they want to bust heads and take names. I realize that there are multiple reasons why a person chooses law enforcement as a career. I was one of the people who chose the career because I simply needed a job. I was 23 years old and about to become a new father. I hadn't graduated from college at the time, and the department provided me with a salary that was better than minimum wage, as well as multiple other health and education benefits. And because of the negative experiences I had with police growing up, I saw it as a chance for me to make a difference in how people viewed police.

Being able to identify why a person wants to become an officer may not weed out every person who has less-than-pure motives for being an officer, but it could help avert putting people who have certain predispositions into stressful situations that will lead them to react in harmful ways. I understand that this is easier said than done due to the shortage of qualified people wanting to become officers. If efforts are made to weed people out, departments may not be able to recruit enough qualified people to allow the department to effectively perform its duties. At the time of this writing, there is a national shortage of qualified candidates.

The following is a brief list outlining some of the leading reasons for this shortage:

- Attrition, the gradual reduction in numbers of officers working on the street, is the primary reason that departments are having a hard time keeping adequate numbers of officers on the streets at any given time.
- Younger officers may not have the same desire to work at one place for their entire career as prior generations may have been willing to do.
- Potential officers have more options to consider for employment that don't require them to put their lives on the line.
- Some potential officers don't want to work for the low pay that is associated with policing.
- Whether an officer feels appreciated or fulfilled within the job also affects whether they will remain with a particular department.

- The overall culture of policing and its requirement that officers fit into a specific type of mold can also be discouraging to potential candidates.
- The increased competition from other types of specialized law enforcement agencies also makes it hard to recruit and keep qualified officers.

Although there is a lot of negative information surrounding why officers are leaving, there is still a certain amount of hope to be found. For many young people who decide to become police officers, they are coming with traits that seem to pave the way for departments to look forward to improved relationships with the public. For some in this new generation of officers, those born after the 1970s, they are less likely to have overtly racists views than prior generations. They do "not have the same personal, contextual background that the older generation may have in understanding law enforcement's historical role in enforcing and reinforcing laws resulting in racial inequity" (Mentel 2012, 10).

Even with this good news, some would say that, due to their youth and unintentional naivety, they may need to be made aware of the historical reasons for the tension between police and minority communities and how that will affect their ability to perform their job functions.

> Proper training and messaging is therefore critical, as younger officers, perhaps lacking both historical context and interpersonal racism, may not connect past wrongs and present-day unintentional bias with (1) institutional racism, (2) legitimate grievances that the African-American community may hold against policing or the criminal justice system as a whole, (3) the legitimacy of their role in navigating the complicated and challenging relationship between the police and citizens of color, and (4) why the community may maintain the incorrect but plausible belief that the police are carrying out a calculated and racist conspiracy. (Mentel 2012, 10)

An additional challenge to this is that although they may not hold racist attitudes like prior generations, they are still operating within an overall system that was not designed to treat all people fairly, whether that is because of racial or economic considerations. Therefore, they may still interact with citizens from a negative standpoint, even though it may not be due to racial considerations.

> Young officers today are not racists; yet they are behaving in exactly the same way, so that people in the community think they are still part of this deliberate attack on them. This does not mean that the police are exhibiting the same racist behavior and attitudes as those from generations ago; however, law enforcement strategies, performance incentives, and tactics have not changed to keep pace with changing attitudes about race and reconciliation. Enforcement-heavy, arrest-driven policing will continue to reinforce the community's belief in police illegitimacy, regardless of whether the young

officer making those arrests considers himself or herself a racist. (Mentel 2012, 11)

The following are suggestions directly geared to law enforcement:

- Departments can invest in a process that seeks to help officers locate and take advantage of resources to help them cope with the stresses of the job.

- Police departments should actively work to counteract the negative stigmas that are placed on officers who do eventually feel burned out by all that they experience.

- Departments must figure out ways for officers to report other officers who commit crimes.

- Law enforcement agencies can stop only rewarding officers for gaining big statistics in certain categories.

- Citizen on patrol academy or a citizens police academy should be offered on a consistent basis.

- Political officials and department commanders should invite regular everyday people from the community to serve in community-based leadership positions within departments instead of political appointees who are being rewarded for supporting politicians during election seasons.

- Police departments need to take the time to add cultural sensitivity training to their requirements for officers on the street and in the academy. (Carter 2015, 31–38)

Fifth, we need to recognize that the relationship between citizens and police is not only shaped by the actions and attitudes they hold and display but is also affected by those who hold political power and use this relationship as a tool to help them gain political office and wield power over everyone's lives. The first thing politicians should do is stop making the process of locking people up and keeping them incarcerated so lucrative. Anyone who is familiar with the inner workings of the legal system knows that the system is all about business—big business.

As was similar to the days following the end of the Civil War, corporations need bodies in order to make profits. Bodies making and delivering the company product. The goal is to have the cheapest bodies making the product in order for the company to reap the highest profits. And like companies after the Civil War, companies have decided that the best bodies for this task are primarily incarcerated bodies. Back then it was slaves. Today it is prisoners.

Prison labor has its roots in slavery. After the 1861–1865 Civil War, a system of "hiring out prisoners" was introduced in order to continue the slavery tradition. Freed slaves were charged with not carrying out their sharecropping commitments (cultivating someone else's land in exchange for part of the harvest) or petty thievery—which were almost never proven—and were then "hired out" for cotton picking, working in mines and building railroads. (Pelaez 2008)

The process didn't end after the Parchman plantation, a Mississippi state prison that was famous for being the place where civil rights activists were sent to pick cotton, was forced to desegregate and end forced cotton picking by inmates. It was able to move into mainstream operation through the legal directives of multiple presidents on both sides of the aisle. A political desire to not look soft on crime ended up fostering the continuance of a plantation process.

> The prison privatization boom began in the 1980s, under the governments of Ronald Reagan and Bush Sr., but reached its height in the 1990s under William Clinton, when Wall Street stocks were selling like hotcakes. Clinton's program for cutting the federal workforce resulted in the Justice Departments contracting of private prison corporations for the incarceration of undocumented workers and high-security inmates.
>
> After a law signed by Clinton in 1996—ending court supervision and decisions—caused overcrowding and violent, unsafe conditions in federal prisons, private prison corporations in Texas began to contact other states whose prisons were overcrowded, offering "rent-a-cell" services in the CCA prisons located in small towns in Texas. The commission for a rent-a-cell salesman is $2.50 to $5.50 per day per bed. The county gets $1.50 for each prisoner. (Pelaez 2008)

Politicians have even used this process to try to recruit companies to stay or relocate to their cities and states in order to take advantage of the cheap prison labor costs.

> [Former] Oregon State Representative Kevin Mannix recently urged Nike to cut its production in Indonesia and bring it to his state, telling the shoe manufacturer that "there won't be any transportation costs; we're offering you competitive prison labor (here)." (Pelaez 2008)

I wonder if Mannix ran on a platform of essentially reinstituting slave labor as a way to bolster economic growth within the state!

Although many people have known that this practice has been in effect for several years, national attention was brought to this practice through popular books and subsequent television shows like *Orange Is the New Black*. This practice is no longer a dirty little secret. Locking people up and keeping them confined makes for lucrative business. Unfortunately, it has become a cottage industry with franchises regularly welcoming new investors. The growth of the industry doesn't seem to be nearing its end anytime soon.

Politicians and little-known companies funded by dark money aren't the only ones benefitting from this practice. Companies that are household names have benefited from the process for a long time as well. Microsoft, Boeing, Texas Instruments, Hewlett-Packard, Macy's, Target, Nordstrom's, Whole Foods, and multiple other companies that we depend on for our daily necessities depend on cheap prison labor to produce the products we want and need.

Because criminals are dehumanized, there really is no incentive for people or companies to change their practices. As long as politicians are elected for preying on the public's general concern about crime, such as all Mexicans are criminals, and receive mountainous financial contributions from lobbyists who work for the prison privatization industry, they will continue to see the process of criminalizing and imprisoning certain people as a valuable plank in the election platforms.

Another suggestion for elected officials is to either end the War on Drugs or at least rethink how it is conducted. Although I am making this suggestion, I'm not saying that we shouldn't seek to try to curb drug use and drug sales. I'm not "pro" drugs or drug dealers. I think that, at its core, the War on Drugs originally was well intentioned. Although it may have begun with the best intentions, in practice, it has had long-term effects that have disproportionately affected minority groups. In practice, it has become yet another tool to disadvantage one community by labeling them as criminals, while other communities are labeled as victims.

> A critical fact often lost in the public debate over the propriety of the nation's "war on drugs" is that the available statistical data suggests that Whites, Latina/os, Blacks, and Asian-Americans have roughly similar rates of illicit drug use. Nonetheless, the "war on drugs" as it has been enforced has had devastating impacts on minority communities across the United States.
>
> Some have labeled the drug war as the "new" Jim Crow, tapping into memories of a long period in U.S. history when criminal laws buttressed racial segregation and served as a bulwark of white supremacy. (Johnson 2010, 1046)

The War on Drugs has not been conducted in a manner that acknowledges the similar rates of drug use and drug sales that occur across all spectrums of our nation. Instead, it has been framed in a way that seeks punishment for the drug culture that is found in minority communities but then seeks understanding and treatment for the drug culture that is found in white communities.

> In fighting the drug war, federal, state, and local law enforcement agencies developed profiles to identify likely offenders. Police in their investigatory activities commonly employed drug courier and gang member profiles, which almost invariably directed law enforcement attention toward

African-American and Latino youth. Racial profiling of young African-American and Latino men in traffic stops on the American roads and highways emerged as a central law enforcement tool in the "war on drugs." Police regularly stop and search Blacks and Latina/os in larger numbers than their percentage of the general population. (Johnson 2010, 1046–1047)

As I have previously stated, this disparity is evidenced by how penalties for similar crimes are different based on whether the crime is considered to be a black crime versus a white crime and the pretexts used to identify potential drug users or dealers. We don't view drug use the same. Crack addiction, which is typically associated with poor minority communities, is labeled despicable and punishable, but heroin and other opioid abuse, which is usually associated with white communities, is labeled a public health concern that can only be fixed by providing greater resources for compassionate education and therapy. Drug crimes are not pursued or enforced equally either. Drug crimes typically committed by minorities are the ones that receive the longest sentences. Almost at a 3:1 percentage, which is similar to the disparities found in how minorities are stopped and ticketed for traffic and lower-level violations.

When elected officials focus on the crimes that typically fit the projected profile of minority groups, policing and punishing those groups become the general focus of the nation. Typically, white citizens then believe that it's not only acceptable but necessary to police those groups in ways that are different from how they themselves are policed. This then can lead to unintended consequences.

> Once government embraces the use of race-based statistical probabilities as a law enforcement tool, the argument logically follows that the probabilities justify similar law enforcement techniques across the board—from combating terrorism to fighting crime on the streets to apprehending undocumented immigrants. (Johnson 2010, 1072)

Even if you don't believe the War on Drugs started as another attempt to criminalize minority communities, that is how it has come to be viewed by many in those communities. What is needed is a consistently open discussion about what it has gotten wrong, what it has gotten right, and how to fix the initiative.

Police and politicians have to take citizen complaints seriously and provide citizens with a mechanism that allows them to make complaints about police actions without fear of reprisal from police, or that their complaint won't simply be ignored because no one wants to do anything about it. Although many departments have offices where citizens can file complaints about officer actions, citizens generally don't believe those complaints are taken seriously, especially when an officer comes back to a citizen who has made a complaint and tells them they will be punished for complaining about them. One thing that could help soothe citizen feelings in this area is for a department to consistently collect data surrounding complaints related to police actions, including but not limited to deadly-force incidents. In order to ensure that information is understood and able to be compared, a standard reporting policy should be developed and instituted.

> For example, many police departments keep records of the number of people shot by police each year, and some track even the number of times police guns are discharged. But departments across the country categorize and track police-involved shootings in different ways, while other uses of physical coercion, even some that are deadly (such as deliberate ramming of vehicles during police chases), may not be tracked at all. Meanwhile, the data on the use of deadly force that police departments provide to the Justice Department under the Uniform Crime Reporting system is provided voluntarily, and differences in reporting procedures across departments seriously limit the comparability of the data. (Lawrence 2000, 25)

By doing this, law enforcement and citizens can consistently compare and contrast information across multiple years, as well as multiple locations, instead of trusting departments will report information that may not always portray them in the best light.

A final suggestion for both law enforcement and elected officials is even if they don't think it's necessary to apologize for past actions committed by police against minority groups, at least publicly acknowledge when an incident does occur that they understand there may be confusion or frustration on the part of minorities. In addition, if they're going to make a statement about the incident, focus on the actions of the incident, not the perceived character of the minority involved, because that makes it seem like law enforcement will seek to find any means to discredit minorities and exonerate police.

An incident that recently occurred at the time of this writing serves as an example. In the early morning hours of September 6, 2018, white Dallas police officer Amber Guyer entered an apartment rented by a black male named Botham Jean. Guyer stated that she thought it was her apartment, and after encountering Botham, she thought he was an intruder. She then shot and killed Botham. She then called 911, and other officers and department officials responded to the scene. Many people believe that's when the coverup of the incident began.

It began with attempts to besmirch Botham's character. Botham was educated, successfully building a career in the finance industry, was a leader within his church, and had never had a run-in with law enforcement. Instead of acknowledging those traits and accomplishments, the Dallas PD obtained a search warrant for Botham's apartment, which led to them finding a small amount of marijuana. This information was leaked to the press. The press shared it. The response in minority communities was, "What does that have to do with an officer shooting him in his own home?"

The release of this information only corroborated the belief that police will go to any lengths to smear a minority instead of acknowledging that one of their own did something wrong. It was also telling that police released the information about the small amount of marijuana found in Botham's apartment but didn't release information related to the toxicology report completed on Guyer's blood that fateful day. This type of incident, a police officer shooting a minority who lived an upstanding life under cloudy circumstances, has happened multiple times. And each time, law enforcement has tried to damage the minority's reputation by releasing peripheral information about them. This reinforces the idea that even when a minority is the victim of a police action, that police action should be viewed in a more forgiving light because the minority still had the potential to be a criminal, even on a small level.

A final suggestion that is geared to white readers who generally view officers as heroes, regardless of the circumstances they are involved in, is to actively attempt to diversify the interactions you have with minorities. You may be thinking, "This is 2019. I know people from every race. I work with minorities every day. I go to church with people who don't look like me every week. I'm not a Neanderthal." I appreciate that the world is different, and we all have more opportunities to interact with people who are different from us. My response to this is that just because we have more opportunities to interact with people who are different from us doesn't mean we actually understand, appreciate, or trust them, because many of our beliefs about other people are influenced by what we see on TV or receive through social media.

Even though you work and worship with minorities, do you live in close proximity to them? Do you have a relationship with them that is more than simply formal or professional? Do you interact with them in ways that allows you to learn about them, their concerns, their hopes and dreams, their fears, and what they have experienced with law enforcement? Or does your relationship with them primarily occur from a position of power, or a position of you having and delivering resources, or in spaces that primarily make sure you are comfortable with the interaction? Simply living in a community that may have two or three black families is not the same as having minorities as personal friends.

I write this because of a troubling trend that seemed to start in 2018. There were a series of events that gained national attention when police were regularly being called on blacks because a white person didn't think that black person belonged in that public space. Whether it was at institutions of higher education, Starbucks, or a golf course, the problem seemed to be that the black people involved were exhibiting a behavior that the white person had a problem with. Whether it was taking a nap in the public area of a dorm room, sitting down before buying coffee, playing golf too slowly, staying at an Airbnb and other residents thinking a black guest couldn't afford to stay there, or students shopping for prom outfits and a store clerk not thinking they could afford to buy anything in the store.

For whites, the actions of the callers may not seem like a big deal. But to blacks, they seem similar to the days when blacks were forced to endure regular separation from whites, whether it was separate lunch counters, dressing rooms, or bathrooms.

> When looking at the incidents that have occurred over the past month, one thing that stands out is how minor some of the alleged offenses are—and that someone feeling suspicious or uncomfortable is enough to warrant calling law enforcement.
>
> These examples show how people of color are subject to arbitrary social expectations and heightened scrutiny. And it's a phenomenon that academics argue is more likely to happen in places where people of color, especially black people, are in the minority. (Lockhart)

The other scary thing about these incidents is the willingness to try to weaponize the police against blacks simply because the callers thought they were up to no good. Was it their actions that made them look like they were up to no good? Or was it their mere presence that set the callers on edge? How many times have the callers observed other white people exhibiting the same behavior but not called police to have that person escorted from the premises? We will never get the answer, but it makes me wonder if this will be a continuing trend.

Historically, whites don't have to change to make blacks comfortable. It's the other way around. Blacks are very aware of the image many whites have about them. In order to make sure whites are comfortable with them and that they don't do anything to accidently verify a preconceived idea about them, they often do what they can to adopt the social and professional norms of whites. Again, many times this is done so they don't bring undue attention and potential negative consequences to themselves.

I did this even when I worked as an officer. When I wasn't in uniform, I always made sure that if I was around white people I didn't know, I automatically introduced myself as "Officer Carter" so they would know that I was "okay" and not a threat to them. I carried my badge on my belt so I could quickly show it to them as proof. I didn't carry it in my back pocket because I didn't want anyone accusing me of reaching for something that could be used to hurt them.

Even today, as a professor and pastor in white settings, I'm still aware that when people meet me for the first time, I have to quickly make sure they know that I'm "okay." I don't speak loudly, don't make quick movements, and try to dress in a way that doesn't make me look like the typical thug that is regularly shown on television. I do this even when I'm playing golf, my favorite activity. I have a white friend from church who I play with on a regular basis. His life experience is totally different from mine. After engaging with him about my understanding of how many white people may perceive me, he acknowledged that he notices that when we walk into the clubhouse to pay for our golf game, which is usually primarily occupied by older white men, they stare at me like they are wondering why I'm there.

White people also have to realize that the black experience isn't uniform anymore. We live and operate in worlds that were off limits to us just 25 years ago. (Again, I'm the pastor of a historically white congregation and I teach at a historically white religious institution with only two full-time black faculty members.) But just because blacks have been able to accomplish certain things in life doesn't mean that people, in particular law enforcement, still don't view us from a particular lens or set of experiences. Being upwardly mobile may give us access to new experiences, but that doesn't shield us from old stereotypes that are entrenched in systems that were designed to keep us in certain places, both physically and socially.

A way to help whites and blacks combat this process that's still in effect is to intentionally build relationships across races and social classes. This is not always easy and is not primarily the responsibility of whites alone, but they hold the power when it comes to questions and conversations of racial reconciliation.

> Whites do not talk about racism because they do not have to talk about it. They have most of the power in the world—economic, political, social, cultural, intellectual, and religious. There is little that blacks and other people of color can do to change the power relations in the churches, seminaries, and society. Powerful people do not talk, except on their own terms and almost never at the behest of others. All the powerless can do is to disrupt— make life uncomfortable for the ruling elites. (Cone 2012, 344)

Whites not only don't have to talk about race, they don't have to talk about how the pursuit of criminality affects blacks because it doesn't primarily affect you. My hope is that after reading this book more of you will.

While I do want to acknowledge those who have joined with blacks to begin to address the disparities in how justice is or isn't administered in appropriate ways, I still have to acknowledge that things will not change until more whites understand the story that has been told about black criminality. I understand that many will push back against what I just stated, citing the election of Barack Obama as our nation's first black president as evidence that race relations have improved in America and that my argument is flawed. Unfortunately, electing a black president didn't result in the incarceration levels of blacks decreasing. Those numbers didn't experience significant change during Obama's eight years in office.

Also, since Obama left office and was replaced by Donald Trump, our nation has experienced an increase in the boldness of white supremacist rhetoric, the building of a substantial physical wall because people agreed with Trump's rhetoric that Mexicans are dangerous and only send their criminals to America, and increased incidents like the one that occurred in Charlottesville, Virginia. In order for our criminal justice system to change, we all have to acknowledge how it has affected vast populations in many intended and unintended ways and that it will take our combined efforts to change it for the better.

My final suggestion is that we must hold reporters and media entities accountable for how they use race to scare others and facilitate some of the divisions that exist in our nation. We must also hold ourselves accountable for how we allow media to think for us instead of thinking for ourselves. "If change is to come about, media outlets need to start facilitating conversations about race and crime in the 21st century. Perhaps journalists should face their own personal biases and/or understand that words have meaning before using racist language in their headlines" (Frisby 2017, 176).

In stating this, I realize that some believe that the media only shows images of blacks as criminals, while others believe that the media doesn't tell the truth about how blacks do participate in criminal behavior. If the only place you get your information about people who are different from you is through the media, you are missing out on what the real world is like. You are missing out on experiencing relationships that may cause you to have to leave your comfort zone, but the places they will take you and the experiences you will have will help contribute to making our nation and world a better place.

This idea is not new. The suggestion to learn who people really are and not just accept what other people tell you to believe about them is found throughout the history of literature. It's found in the book *The Adventures of Huckleberry Finn*, which was written by Mark Twain, and the corresponding musical *Big River*. The book and musical chronicle the adventures of two boys, Huckleberry Finn and Tom Sawyer, and a runaway slave named Jim and their adventures along the Mississippi River during the late nineteenth century.

In the story, Huck has been adopted by two older women, and they set out to civilize him and save his soul. Huck dreams of adventure and love. Jim, the slave, dreams of equality, freedom, and opportunity. Although they are worlds apart, they have a common hope: to be free. To be free of others' expectations of them. To be free of the physical confines they both face. Within the story, Huck and Jim encounter questions, questions that are generated from outside parties and questions that come from within themselves. Questions like, "Is life fair?" "Did God create all people to be equal?" "If God did, why are some people not treated that way?"

Huck, the boy of adventure, also has to deal with the question of whether he's willing to be made into a civilized young man by his aunts and the townspeople. Jim also has to deal with questions: Will he allow himself to continue being treated as "other?" Will he allow himself to be sold to yet another master, who in all likelihood, will not treat him well? Neither wait for someone else to give them the answers to their questions. They both escape their circumstances and begin to float down the Mississippi River toward freedom. Physical and psychological. *Huckleberry Finn* and *Big River* deal with questions. Personal and corporate. The most interesting one to me is, "Do we have to accept the future that someone else has planned for us or others?"

I think another religious text expresses the same idea. Acts 10 deals with these types of questions as well. Are we locked into following older traditions of how we view relationships and interact with people, or with appropriate prompting and blessing, are we allowed to make a new path of what it means to live in relationship with each other? The central characters of the text are forced to address the idea of being worlds apart and with the idea of "otherness." I won't bore the reader by repeating all the details of the text, but I will summarize it as quickly as possible.

In the text we are introduced to Cornelius, a Gentile official within the oppressive Roman army. Cornelius wasn't necessarily a bad man. He actually seems to be a very good man. He was a "God-fearer," and so were the people in his household. He worshipped at the local Jewish synagogue, acknowledged the God of the Jews as the one true God, and complied with some Jewish customs. Although he followed many of the Jewish customs, he likely was not circumcised and would have been considered a good person, but just not good enough. Jewish tradition said he wasn't good enough because he was not a Jew. He was "other."

Cornelius is visited by an angel who tells him that God has recognized his heart and sacrifice. His prayers to God have not been ignored. His gifts on behalf of other people have not been ignored. God recognized and appreciated his actions. He was pleasing to God. The angel then directs Cornelius to send men to Joppa to find a man named Simon Peter. He isn't told why. He's just told to do it. And he complied. The next day, Simon Peter, one of Jesus' former disciples, was sitting on a roof trying to figure out what he wanted for lunch. He suddenly had a vision in which he saw the heavens open and something like a big sheet descend from the sky. On the sheet were all kinds of animals. Birds and reptiles. Big and small.

A voice from heaven commanded Peter to rise, kill, and eat. This was a no-no for Peter, the devout Jew. Throughout his life, he was taught to read the right books, go to the right places, avoid the wrong people, and not eat certain food. To Peter, these animals were not right. They were unclean, defiled, and "other." Before it was all done, the voice told Peter multiple times, "What God has made clean, do not call common." Don't call it defiled or "other." As you can imagine, Peter was mystified and stunned. Why would God ask him to do something that he understood to be sin? Why would God ask him to do something "other?" Something uncomfortable? Before he could come up with an answer, the Spirit of God told him that Gentiles would come looking for him and he should go with them. Shortly thereafter, Cornelius' men arrived looking for Peter and he went with them.

I don't want to gloss over this important series of events. This is a significant development in the life of this devout Jew named Peter and the Roman official named Cornelius. Jews didn't fraternize with Gentiles and vice versa. Cornelius represented Rome's military power and control over Peter's people. Positive casual interaction between Peter and Cornelius would have been unlikely under most circumstances. A devout Jew, in general, would have has very little to do with a Gentile. Having fellowship with a Gentile was like eating unclean meat that came down on a sheet from heaven. Yet there Peter was. In a Gentile's home, doing the unthinkable.

At that meeting, Peter shares his particular faith with all who were gathered, and they were all converted. People who were once considered unclean were found to be acceptable to the same God Peter followed. People who were once considered to be "other" were now part of the same spiritual family. Those whom Peter once called outsiders are now called children of God. This happened not because Peter wanted it to. It happened because Peter's God said that they were acceptable. It was Peter's job to get in line with God's thinking.

People who, at the beginning of the day, were worlds apart became spiritual brothers and sisters. Those who, like Jim and Huck Finn, saw the same stars through different eyes and experiences, those that were worlds apart, were now seeing life the same. Jim and Huck Finn and Peter and Cornelius aren't the only ones who have to deal with this issue of differing worlds or clean versus unclean. We do as well—we just call it something else. Although you may not disregard someone due to their skin color, you likely disregard people for other reasons.

A pastor friend of mine once said that people everywhere call somebody unclean. St. Louis calls Kansas City unclean because of the Royals. St. Louis calls Chicago unclean because of the Cubs and the Blackhawks. We all look for people who we can cast to the outside so we can feel comfortable residing on the inside. My question for the reader is, who helps you feel like an insider? What person or group of people do you stand against in order to help you find your identity? Unfortunately, America has made a history of doing this to black and brown people. What will it take for this to end?

Brief Concluding Thoughts

"If your theology allows you to exclude people in the afterlife, it makes it easier to do the same in the here and now."

—Holy Heretics Podcast, 2018

A story is being told that needs to be addressed. The truth is that black people commit crimes. Black people in Chicago and St. Louis shoot each other on a regular basis. Black people in New York break into cars, steal them, and go on joy rides. Black people in Baltimore sell and smoke crack. White people all over our country do the same thing. But that's not the story that's being told. The story that we're regularly being told is that only, or primarily, blacks are criminals.

When a police officer is accused or found guilty of breaking the law or mistreating black and brown citizens, the media and white citizens say that officer was a bad officer or an outlier, implying that the officer was acting in a way that wasn't normal for the culture of policing. But when an African American is accused or convicted of wrongdoing, the assumptions and statements are that person represents all black people. We never hear that they are a bad singular person. Instead, they represent all people like them.

I know that black people shoot and rob each other, steal cars, and use drugs. It's a fact that can't be denied. Criminal behavior is a part of black life. But that's not the only experience of black people. The story that's being told implies that this type of behavior forms the foundation for much of black life. That isn't true. Black people who participate in this type of behavior are in the minority. Just as in white, Asian, Latino, or any other culture. The story implies that black criminality is much worse and more pervasive than the criminality of any other group of people. We can no longer believe this story.

The formation and sharing of this story weren't by accident. It was done intentionally by a small group of people who hoped that people in our country wouldn't be savvy enough to decipher bad information or were not inclined to ask more questions when they heard the story told. Unfortunately, in many ways their plan was successful. In our nation, we have an image in our minds of who black people are and how they act that has been passed down from generation to generation. We allow a few incidents to represent an entire group of people and their existence.

The story may show that black criminality is real, but it doesn't show that black criminality doesn't exist solely because black people hold a disposition toward crime. Data may show that some blacks do have extensive criminal histories and serve longer prison terms due to those histories, but their initial introduction to the criminal justice system may have been due to the attitudes, misconceptions, and illegal and immoral actions of those who are charged with protecting and serving them. The story may show that whites' views of blacks have improved over the years, but long-held beliefs about black culture and the need for white culture to be protected from its growth and intrusion into their daily lives insulates whites from understanding or acknowledging their participation in furthering the story.

As I understand it, law enforcement, the main antagonist in this story, in and of itself, isn't the only problem. The systems that continue to make unnecessary distinctions between people of different skin colors and socioeconomic statuses are responsible culprits as well. Until we can figure out ways to see the common value we all intrinsically hold and see police as the servants of our common good, including good that equally incorporates black and brown people, we will continue to live within a nation that will go to any means to keep certain people within their designated places. We all must understand and acknowledge our part in the system and the story that is being told if we hope to change it for the better.

A final religious text will help me clarify this idea. In the biblical book of Jonah, God calls a prophet to participate in the process of redeeming a certain group of people. The problem was this group was the mortal enemy of Jonah's tribe. The last thing he wanted was to do anything nice for them. He would have preferred to witness their city burning to the ground with all of them in it. Jonah was fighting mad that God would want something good to happen for them. He was even madder that his God was asking him to do it.

I understand Jonah's frustration. In the neighborhood where I grew up with my twin brother, enemies were commonplace and fighting was an expected part of life. Not a pleasantly expected part of life, but a part, nonetheless. Knowing that physical altercations were going to be a part of life, my grandparents tried to mentally prepare us for the days that we would find ourselves in the unfortunate position of having to physically defend ourselves. Part of that preparation was to instill in us the mind-set that we were to never start a fight, but we sure were supposed to try to end it by beating the other person—and if we couldn't beat them, that person should at least walk away knowing that they had been in a fight.

My grandparents were both faithful, loving Christians who took us to church twice a week. As much as they taught us the value of memorizing and living out Christian principles, they also taught us to value our own safety and to protect ourselves from unnecessary physical harm. For them, it was one of the realities they knew we would face, and they wanted us to have a plan for handling the tough parts of life. They knew that although we were Christians, we didn't live in a vacuum. Just because they were teaching us to live in a certain way didn't mean that other parents were teaching their children the same thing.

This idea of not living in a vacuum is still true today. Just because I believe certain things about life doesn't mean anyone else in the world respects or agrees with my beliefs and values. I believe in unconditional love, the inherent value of all life, and that all people were created in the image of a common Creator and therefore hold certain intrinsic values. The truth is that not everyone sees value in all lives. Unfortunately, some people see just the opposite. They see value not in recognizing and respecting life, but in taking it and hurting it. We are reminded of this every time we hear about a mass shooting, or terrorist act, or some other senseless act of violence that changes people's lives unnecessarily.

In Jonah 4, our antihero is angry at God because God sent him to preach repentance to the people of Nineveh who, in the not-so-distant past, had conducted terrorist strikes against Jonah's people, the Israelites, and defeated them. Nineveh was the sworn enemy of Jonah's people, and God had the nerve to send him to those people so they could be saved. Think about that for a moment. It would be like a person who lost a loved one in a terrorist attack being sent by God to a terrorist training camp and having that person say to everyone at the camp, "Repent because God wants you to be forgiven and reconciled to Him." Can you imagine how much pain and confusion that person would be facing?

Jonah's faith and theology didn't exist within a vacuum. Neither did his pain or his frustration with God or the people of Nineveh. Jonah expressed this anger toward God. He told God that he didn't want to see the Ninevites repent because he knew that God would forgive them if they did. The last thing Jonah wanted to see was them receiving the same thing from God that he and Israel had received, which was forgiveness. He knew that there would be consequences to preaching to the people of Nineveh. Either they would disregard him and die, or they would believe him and continue to live.

God's response to Jonah's protest was a simple question: "Don't you think I should be concerned about those people?" I leave the reader with the same type of question. Shouldn't we be concerned about all people? Not just those who look like us, or have similar life experiences as we do, or who occupy the same economic strata as us? You don't have to be a person who holds to any religious faith to understand the importance of this. Unless we begin to not only understand this but also live it out, we will continue to be a divided nation sliding down a slippery slope.

Postscripts

Instead of continuing with a lengthy conclusion, I want to end this book by sharing a multipart postscript that I think will help readers better understand the intricacies of how the story that has been told affects even police officers, in particular black officers. The first postscript is a list of articles that have been published in the past few years that share data and information in an accessible way and reinforces the thoughts in this book. Understanding that most readers don't want to have paragraphs of data shoved at them, I share these links in the hopes that they are an easy way for readers to become even more familiar with how police patrol different communities differently, the efforts officers and departments go to to justify or cover up those practices, efforts to besmirch an African American victim's reputation, and the public's defense of officers, even when it has been proven that they have acted wrongly.

The second postscript is an interview I conducted with Detective Sergeant Heather Taylor who is, at the time of this writing, assigned to the Homicide Division for the St. Louis Metropolitan Police Department. She is also the president of the Ethical Society of Police, a primarily African American police officers association with branches serving officers for the St. Louis city and St. Louis County police departments.

The third postscript is a document that outlines the recent work of the Alliance for Interracial Dignity, a volunteer-led group of residents, primarily from Webster Groves, Missouri, who have been intentional in calling local police departments into account for how they spend public funds as it relates to policing local communities. I believe Sgt. Taylor and the leaders of the Alliance for Racial Dignity can serve as models for how the story of black criminality intersects with the system that is policing and eventually bring about positive change.

The final postscript is a spiritual exploration of the idea of Christian responsibility to recognize the inherent value held by those who may be different from us. As you read this, you may wonder why I have decided to include something like this in a nonreligious book that deals with the legal and sociological realities of policing in America. The answer is simple: before I served as a police officer, I served the church. While I was an officer, I served as interim pastor of a congregation located in one of the districts I actively patrolled. After I left the department, I accepted a call to return to that district to serve as lead pastor of a different congregation. While serving there, people who previously only knew me as Officer Carter visited the church. I eventually began to build relationships with people I had previously arrested in ways I had never imagined. Those relationships were built on a common foundation of faith.

I am a person of faith. I am unashamed about that fact. But I also respect that not everyone believes what I believe or agrees with the idea of maintaining religious beliefs. With that being said, I can't get away from my faith. It is what causes me to believe that all people are created equal and deserve to be treated with value. Unfortunately, those of us who claim to have particular faith practices as a shared background spend an awful lot of time looking like our faith has been influenced by the world and politics, instead of the other way around. Whether you're a person of faith or not, I invite you to read those words and consider them. If they don't hold any meaning for you, I hope you will consider sharing them with someone for whom they may hold meaning.

Postscript #1

A Brief History of Slavery and the Origins of American Policing

https://plsonline.eku.edu/insidelook/brief-history-slavery-and-origins-american-policing

A short academic article that relates the connection between the birth of policing in the United States and its connection to maintaining slavery's presence in certain geographic areas.

United States Department of Justice Civil Rights Division. 2015. Investigation of the Ferguson Police Department

https://www.justice.gov/sites/default/files/opa/press-releases/attachments/2015/03/04/ferguson_police_department_report.pdf

The report from the Department of Justice concerning the investigation into illegal behaviors utilized by police officers and the legal system in Ferguson, Missouri, against African American and poor community members.

African American Male Police Officers' Perceptions of Being Racially Profiled by Fellow Police Officers

https://scholarworks.waldenu.edu/dissertations/3434/

This accessible 2017 doctoral dissertation explored the experiences of black police officers who were racially profiled during traffic stops by their white co-workers.

Race and the Tragedy of Quota-Based Policing
http://prospect.org/article/race-and-tragedy-quota-based-policing-0
(The article originally appeared in *The American Prospect* magazine.)
Extensive 2016 article exploring the pervasiveness of police arrest and citation quotas that are still in practice and how they primarily affect black and brown and poorer citizens.

4 St. Louis Police Officers Indicted, Accused of Beating an Undercover Colleague during Stockley Protests
https://www.stltoday.com/news/local/crime-and-courts/st-louis-police
-officers-indicted-accused-of-beating-an-undercover/article_4a82d209
-b3cd-565e-9a97-309cf1c2a5af.html
In 2017, four St. Louis police officers working a detail related to public protests of the exoneration of a white officer who had been filmed pursuing and killing a black suspected drug dealer beat multiple protestors, one of which turned out to be a black undercover St. Louis officer.

For Framing Innocent Black Men, a Florida Police Chief Gets 3 Years in Prison
https://www.miamiherald.com/news/local/community/miami-dade
/article222205540.html
In 2018, the police chief of Biscayne Park, Florida, was convicted of directing his officers to arrest black men who didn't look like they belonged in the area and to charge them with burglary so the department could keep its burglary clearance rate at 100 percent. One of the ironies in this case is the chief's prison sentence was shorter than the sentence given to some of the men who were falsely accused of burglary and other crimes.

Why Did Dallas Police Search a Man's Home for "Narcotics" after One of Their Own Killed Him?
https://reason.com/blog/2018/09/12/frfrfr
As previously shared, in 2018, a white female officer in Dallas, Texas, assuming it was her residence, entered the wrong apartment and killed the occupant. Instead of acting and communicating transparently about what occurred, the Dallas department obtained a search warrant in the hopes of finding illegal contraband. They found a small amount of marijuana and leaked this information to reporters in the hopes that it would help them frame the victim in a negative way, all the while never answering the question of why the officer was still employed by them after she killed someone who was in their own home.

New Jersey Sheriff Resigns after Racist Remarks Captured on Tape
https://thehill.com/blogs/blog-briefing-room/news/407831-nj-sheriff
-resigns-after-racist-remarks-captured-on-tape
   In 2018, a New Jersey sheriff and multiple deputies resigned after tape surfaced of the sheriff making disparaging comments in line with his belief that there is a propensity for criminal behavior in African American communities and the lack of adequate criminal prosecution in his community.

Rioting Eagles Fans Prove White Privilege Is Alive and Well
http://faithfullymagazine.com/philly-riots-eagles-fans-white-privilege/
   In 2018, the Philadelphia Eagles won the Super Bowl. Primarily white fans responded by participating in public riots and mass destruction of public property. The article reflects on how these actions were framed in a positive way due to whites being the primary perpetrators versus how the actions would have been perceived had the groups been primarily African American.

Postscript #2

WHY DOES THE ETHICAL SOCIETY OF POLICE EXIST?

Interview for the *Communities Forward* podcast, recorded September 3, 2016.

Terrell Carter (TC): Good afternoon, this is Terrell Carter and I am your host for *Communities Forward. Communities Forward* is a program that seeks to move communities forward through conversations with community leaders, and to figure out ways to help improve our communities, help improve our neighborhoods, and to help improve our region. Today we have a special guest with us. Her name is Sergeant Heather Taylor, and she is the president of the Ethical Society of Police. The Ethical Society of Police is the African American Police Officers' Association for the city of St. Louis, and in a moment of transparency, or a moment of clarity, I just have to remind everyone that I am a former St. Louis city police officer. I was a police officer for five years. I did not have the pleasure of working with Sergeant Taylor, but I'm very familiar with some of the concerns, or some of the things that she sees on a daily basis, and I hope this will be an interesting conversation. Sergeant Taylor, thank you for joining us today.

Sergeant Taylor (HT): Thank you for having me.

Terrell Carter: So, I always like to begin the program by asking our guests just to tell our listeners about themselves, so they can understand who you are and some of your life experience. Are you from St. Louis? Did you grow up in St. Louis?

Sergeant Taylor: Yes, born and raised here.

Terrell Carter: Is there a particular neighborhood that you grew up in?

Sergeant Taylor: The Greater Ville and Ville neighborhoods.

Terrell Carter: For our listeners who may not be familiar with the Greater Ville and the Ville neighborhood, which is where I grew up as well, right behind Sumner High School, would you explain what the Ville is, and as I ask that question, I have a big smile on my face. Explain to our listeners what the Ville is.

Sergeant Taylor: The Ville is in north St. Louis, a predominantly African American neighborhood. It's the corridors, I want to say, and hopefully I get them right because they did the redistricting thing that was a nightmare, it's going to be, I believe, Cook to Vandeventer, Vandeventer no—Vandeventer to Kingshighway north and south streets, Cook east and west to . . .

Terrell Carter: The big thing is, it's in north St. Louis.

Sergeant Taylor: Yes, it's in north St. Louis.

Terrell Carter: And physically, economically, what is the Ville like? The Greater Ville?

Sergeant Taylor: It's doing a come-up. They're building and trying to revitalize the area, and it's looking good. But it's predominantly African American, lower income, you know the one school there of course is going to be Sumner High School.

Terrell Carter: And they've tried to close Sumner how many times?

Sergeant Taylor: Oh, numerous!

Terrell Carter: They're both neighborhoods, or both communities, that need help . . . I'm sorry. "Help" is not the word. Attention.

Sergeant Taylor: Resources.

Terrell Carter: Resources, right. And this interview is not about the distribution of resources in the city of St. Louis. I'm waiting for a different conversation, or different day for that, but it's a challenge I can imagine, it was a challenge growing up in that area. It was a joy for us. I say us because I have a twin brother. It was a joy for us because we didn't know any better. Do you still live in north St. Louis? I'm not asking for your address. But do you still live in the city of St. Louis?

Sergeant Taylor: I did when I first became a police officer. For about four years, I stayed in the Ville area. I moved to Central Patrol, and I live south now.

Terrell Carter: Okay. So, why did you become a police officer?

Sergeant Taylor: You know, I've always loved uniform. I actually wanted to be a Marine. That was like one of my very first goals in life was to join the Marine Corps. And I had a cousin who joined the police department, she was a Marine, and she also was a St. Louis City police officer and detective. We were always taught to respect the police and to obey the law and to do right, and we had a brother who didn't do those things, and so we saw the interactions that happened with my . . . I'm the youngest, but my brother, who's the second youngest . . . got in trouble a lot. There were good cops and then there were some bad ones. The good cops showed me how things should be, and I always respected that. I was just in awe of it. And I wanted to become a police officer from that standpoint. But in 1992, my aunt was shot and killed by a St. Louis city sheriff's deputy, and he received . . . which was my cousin, my cousin was a police officer who was still on the department at the time, and he was arrested, and he received a very light sentence. And from that day forward, I knew that I would ultimately become a police officer. It's all I wanted to do. I went away to school on a basketball scholarship to Southern Illinois University, but I only wanted to be a police officer. I wanted to go into it to change it and to be like those officers who were nice to my brother despite, even though he was pretty bad, despite him being bad, they treated him nice. They treated my family nice despite his actions which were very wrong.

Terrell Carter: For me, that's not unique. In our neighborhood, and again I didn't ask what specific street you lived on, we lived behind Sumner. And again, Sumner is the oldest black high school in the city of St. Louis, and not just the city of St. Louis but in the region if I'm not mistaken.

Sergeant Taylor: I think so.

Terrell Carter: Okay. There was a lot of action that occurred around there, and our experiences with police were not necessarily positive at all. We did have one, no we had two, positive police influences in our lives when we were younger. One, a lieutenant named Glenn Williams. I don't know if you ever had the chance to work with him?

Sergeant Taylor: No.

Terrell Carter: Okay, so, we met Glenn through his son. When we were kids, we went to Marshall Elementary, and then we went to Simmons Middle School. But the point is we grew up with his son, and then the captain of the 8th District, that's the district it was at the time, was a black man and I forget his name right now, but he coached my uncles. But the other police officers that we knew, that we met, we did not have such positive relationships with. I find it interesting, and thankful on your behalf, that you had those positive interactions with police when you were young. How long have you been on the department now?

Sergeant Taylor: Sixteen years.

Terrell Carter: If I was still there, I would be two years away from retiring.

Sergeant Taylor: Four years away.

Terrell Carter: In your 16 years . . . well, let me back up and ask this question: What did you expect when you became a police officer, or did you have any expectations?

Sergeant Taylor: I was very naïve. My expectations were that I was going to just meet people, and I was going to change their lives and I was going to save everyone's life and kumbaya and hug and it was going to be great. And you know, a lot of times it really has been that way. But that was my expectation. Even though we lived in north St. Louis in an area where crack cocaine use and crime just exploded, we were still very sheltered. I'd never seen things and coming from college and being so green . . . you know, I just had different expectations. And actually, I still kind of do believe that some of those things, they will happen.

Terrell Carter: You still believe that what things will happen?

Sergeant Taylor: That I will continue to change policing and continue to be a positive influence with police work.

Terrell Carter: Over the 16 years, how has the department changed? I know that's a very broad question. What I'm trying to get people to understand, is that policing obviously is . . . I think everyone knows that policing is not an easy job, to say the least. But policing is not just about putting on your uniform and going outside and interacting with citizens. Fortunately, or unfortunately, there are a lot of things that go on behind the scene that influence how you can do your job . . . that affect your ability to do certain things. In general, or in specifics, how has your department changed in 16 years?

Sergeant Taylor: I think our department has changed in the sense that we are so much about enforcement, and you know enforcement . . . if you look at crime, crime is out of control. Enforcement is . . . yeah, there's a great need for enforcement. But that community-oriented policing aspect, police athletically (referring to the Police Athletic Leagues) . . . it's here, but it's not like it was when I first started. When I first started, I coached basketball. So, I was very involved. There were a lot of coaches, different sports. We all had these teams. We were able to connect with kids and just follow their progress. And now? It's different. I haven't coached in eight years, maybe, or somewhere around there. And police athletically, things like that are the community-oriented aspects of policing. You had the officers in schools. You had officers in just about every other school, and now you don't have that. There are less officers, of course, but the connections with people and connecting to people is gone. People have to trust you to tell you about crime. They really just have to. There's a lack of trust, and a lot of it came about because of the actions of bad officers. There's a huge disconnect now compared to the way it was when I first started. I'm not saying that things were great when I first came on in 2000, but now things are just . . . there's a huge divide, you know?

Terrell Carter: There's a huge divide between citizens and police?

Sergeant Taylor: Absolutely. There's a huge divide between citizens and police. The trust factor is much less. Not that it was some outstanding factor anyway, but it's much less than it was when I first started. Gone are the days of chasing someone with a gun and running through (a neighborhood) and people telling you, "Hey! There he is! He went that way! He went that way!" Those days are very few. Those things don't happen a lot, compared to when I first started. The things that you see. . . . Some of it, no, a lot of it, is in the hands of officers because of a lack of trust.

Terrell Carter: What are some of the most crucial things facing St. Louis from a law enforcement perspective?

Sergeant Taylor: Just . . . the stuff we just spoke about. The disconnect between the community, our ability to have people trust us . . . to tell us what's happening in communities to solve crimes. We are so much about enforcement. I'm not trying to say that enforcement isn't critical. It IS. But there are times where you have an opportunity to connect with someone. Every day, any of us driving or doing anything, we're probably committing a crime. But what crimes are worth arresting for? Some crimes just aren't worth arresting. When you have the opportunity to change the landscape of someone's life. If you put them in jail, is it really going to solve the issue for some crime that's victimless? There has to be more of a . . . there is a need for, the community-oriented policing cop philosophy more so. I believe now, more than ever, because we're so disconnected.

Terrell Carter: How do commanders respond to that kind of thinking? The reason why I ask is. . . . So, I left the police department because I testified against my partner. Now, I'll never say that I was a perfect police officer. I am a Christian. I am a pastor. The point is, even within the faith system that I have, it was hard for me to walk according to that system and do the daily job of being a police officer. I'm not making excuses. I'm just saying that's a reality. And I imagine that's some of the struggle that you may go through, and other officers go through. In my heart and in my mind, I wanted to do the things that you just talked about. Most people, as you said, don't know, or don't realize that, from the time they start their car and the time they drive to the first stop sign in their neighborhood, they've probably committed a couple violations and could get tickets for that. But what's the point of making somebody's life harder when you can take a few moments to educate them? And you don't know what's going on or what has happened to them since they woke up that morning. My sergeants, my lieutenants did not care about that particular kind of thinking. It was, "You need to make statistics." Well it really wasn't "I" needing to make statistics. THEY were being told that their men needed to make statistics to make whatever lieutenant happy, to make whatever captain happy, to make whatever major happy . . . whatever. And I understand that because, in a sense, it's somewhat of a business; you have to be able to show why you are employed and that you're doing things in the community, all those things. My point is my philosophy as an officer was closer to yours, and I met a lot of pushback from my superiors. How do you, are you able to, interact with other commanders, because you work in what department?

Sergeant Taylor: Homicide.

Terrell Carter: And what does homicide do?

Sergeant Taylor: We investigate murders.

Terrell Carter: And St. Louis is one of the highest, statistically, cities for which crime?

Sergeant Taylor: We are rated number one per capita for homicide victims.

Terrell Carter: So, your job is not to go out and make people feel good. Your job is to go find out who killed someone.

Sergeant Taylor: It IS to make people feel good in a sense, because we want to give validation. We want our families to feel that, to know that, we are working hard to put somebody in jail that took the life of someone else. That nobody has the right to do that.

Terrell Carter: How do you reconcile . . . no, how do you combine . . . reconcile is not the right word . . . how do you combine . . . how do you get your philosophy to work within the system where you're detailed right now? And when we use the word "detail," that word means where you are stationed. And that detail can change tomorrow. It can change two years from now and you may be in traffic, or you may be back in a regular uniform in the district.

Sergeant Taylor: It's very different for me because I'm in homicide. It's different from being in a specialized unit where you're focused on guns and drugs and things of that nature; where it's stat driven. Homicide is also stat driven, because, of course, you want to solve homicides. At the end of the day, you are giving families some sense of justice. And that's our goal. In that it's different from a victimless crime like dope and drugs, or anything like that. For us, it is driven. You are driven. My crew? I'm a sergeant. I want them ABSOLUTELY driven to solve these crimes because 90 percent of the people who are murdered, they look just like me, and they come from the same backgrounds that I came from: poor, impoverished, a lot of struggles financially, just systemic factors. So yes, we are driven. I'm not driven to put a case on someone (falsely charge someone with a crime in order to pad arrest statistics) that didn't commit murder. No! But we are driven in the sense that we have to help people understand that we can have a homicide victim who could have been on paper (on probation or recently paroled) or have an arrest history a mile long. But, at the end of the day, someone took his or her life and they didn't have a right to do that. That person has a family, they may have kids, there may be that "one" family member that's concerned about us solving that crime . . . that's who we work for. But as far as units where statistics are driven, I've been in specialized units my whole career, where you were focused on violent crime; getting robberies, guns, dope . . . things of that nature that historically are problems within our communities. Am I statistic driven? In a sense yes. I was in those types of units as well. The push, as far as I think when I came on (to the police department), you had the issues where officers were trying to make stats and it was a big, big push with that. But for me? I can tell you I've, even when I started the police academy, run-ins with commanders where I spoke my mind. I've never really ever gotten away from that. Maybe, for me it hasn't hurt (my career) as much as others, but just being able to stand up and speak your mind and tell it like you thought it was and what was right morally and what wasn't (has been important). I've been transferred for speaking my mind. I've been that I would work in prisoner processing for the rest of my career. You name it. I have not been given jobs because "You're not one of us, really." And sometimes it is about corruption and it is about what you're willing to do and what you're not willing to do as a cop. And that's where a LOT of cops run into problems. At the end of the day, you have to remember those oaths that you take to be just and fair. You can't buy into the philosophy of the codes of silence that says, "Oh I'm going to make this arrest" for statistics and things like that. We have certain people we're arresting. This person is probably addicted to crack cocaine. And maybe they have crack on them. But do we really need to tow their car? What is that really resolving? All that's doing is making people hate us. We are towing their car. We're going to lock you up because the drugs are yours. But if you're towing their cars, and you're doing those extra things that aren't necessary? That's when we become disconnected as officers. And that's a huge part of the problem. You're already taking away someone's freedom. And then towing their cars, and when they try to get their car out . . . guess what? It's going to cost you a WHOLE lot of cash to get your car out. We're doing all of these things and what's the purpose? The purpose is to make money. It's about statistics. It's about making money and driving revenue for a lot of areas. Even in the city of St. Louis, we had the towing scandal (that occurred in a specialized unit: Asset Forfeiture). After that, officers don't tow cars now. Well, we shouldn't have been towing cars before because if you think about it, what's the purpose of it? We're taking someone's car. They may have a wife or kid, or whoever, who can use that car to continue to live some form of a normal lifestyle to get to and from work, but we're doing all those things that aren't really necessary. And people can say that, "Oh, it's liberal. It's soft." But really, morally, it's just RIGHT.

Terrell Carter: These people that are being arrested are still human, as well.

Sergeant Taylor: Right. Exactly.

Terrell Carter: One of the challenges that I experienced early on, and this . . . I got over it pretty quickly, or was able to transfer away from that idea, that feeling . . . was that of me being separate from the citizens I was patrolling or from the world that I was working in. You know, seeing people as "other." And you're living it on a daily basis, so I'm not playing the world's smallest violin for myself. . . . The point is that, I recognize that idea. I want to continue to explore this vein of your thinking in a more positive light, I guess. What have been the greatest opportunities to make a difference in people's lives as a police officer? You just talked about the fact that you're in homicide. My mother was killed when I was seven years old. One of the ironies of my tenure as a police officer is that the young police officer who found my mother, I eventually met him never knowing he was the one . . . you know, this is 20 some odd years later, Lieutenant Scego, who is no longer on the police department, but Lieutenant Scego was a patrolman who was the first responder to my mother being killed. I waited until three weeks before I finally quit the department to finally look up her report, and found . . . I was like, "Wow, I worked with the man that showed up to my mother's . . . and you know, went to the hospital and talked with my grandparents . . . all those things." And I wish I could have said thank you to him, if I would have known. And then I had the opportunity to work with his son as well, which is a unique story into itself, but we'll leave that alone. The point is that in the big scheme of things you have such an important position in homicide. But what have been some of the other ways that you've made differences in people's lives just [as] a patrolman or as a sergeant, you know, out in the street?

Sergeant Taylor: Some of those things . . . you just DO THEM. It just is what it is. Somebody's hungry, or somebody needs transportation to get somewhere, you just kind of . . . if you're half a human being, you just do them. Those things are the things that you remember about this job at the end of the day. Victims I've had that have written letters to me. Suspects I've had that have written letters to me thanking me. Those are the things you remember the most about this job. It just stays with you. The push that keeps you going, you know? When you have bad days, or when you are dealing with a command staff that just doesn't get it. Those are the things you remember. Or even more so now, with us, it's like . . . if it wasn't for the community? * deep breath * Man, this struggle . . . this fight right now would be a thousand times worse if we didn't have the community behind us pushing us to be transparent, REALLY transparent, not just saying the word but actually being transparent and standing up against corruption and speaking out against bad officers and bad things that are happening around the country. Those experiences, things people have thanked you for, and the community . . . yeah, without their support I think most of us would be zombies in this place.

Terrell Carter: A few weeks ago, almost a month ago, I saw an article in the primary Chicago newspaper that talked about being a police officer, being a black police officer, and the challenges that go along with that. Do you see, and this is a general question . . . I know you cannot speak for all black police officers. Is that something that is experienced by police officers in the city of St. Louis? And [as] I ask that question, in the back of my mind I think about how, statistically, St. Louis is one of most racially divided cities. The political division that we have, the economic division, the north side versus south side and how all of that plays into effect. . . . Is that a factor as well for police officers? For African American police officers? Or is it just when they put on the uniform, it's all about being blue?

Sergeant Taylor: It's a definite divide. You live it every time, you know, I go out and I'm exposed as a police officer and I show up on scenes. I'm African American first. That's the first thing that I am. And I'm proud to be African American. I love African American people. I love PEOPLE, period, but you know I am an African American female, so when I go to scenes in north St. Louis, these are people. These are people that could have been me, could have been my family, you know it is a difference. And secondly, I'm a police officer. And it's difficult at times because we get the negative, and we get the pushback from our own community, as well, because they don't trust us . . . because so many of us have not stood up. We have, right now, an African American (female) commander, a major, suing the department for gender discrimination. But MAN, we're looking at it like, "Do you not understand? This is about YOU. Do you not understand what's happening with policing right now in this country? In this world? What about the people in the community as an African American major on our police department?" One of the second highest-ranked commander[s] on the police department, and . . .

Terrell Carter: To be a woman?

Sergeant Taylor: Yeah, to be a woman. And this is what you're standing up for? I understand that gender discrimination is huge, just as equally as being oppressed and being African American, those things are huge as well. But as an African American here, you're not speaking on the oppression and the things that are happening in this city and the things that are happening all around the world. We're making . . . we're going out . . . the major is going out and she's speaking about THAT, but what [about] this? What about the blue code of silence? What about that? That's a huge issue. Being African American and a police officer, you feel, especially in our position, unethical. We feel like we have a huge responsibility to stand up, to speak out about oppression for everyone, whether you're white, black, Asian, no matter what your sexual orientation is, your religion; all those things are important. Any form of oppression or maltreatment of someone is huge, especially for law enforcement officers, because we are held to a higher standard. And sometimes it's very difficult when we are going out and policing. I mean, you're called a sellout just because you're a cop. And you have people who don't know you individually, don't know your struggle and probably don't know that you're one of the most (vocal) people on the department (related to) standing up for what's right. And you get it, just because they see (what occurs on the streets and think) "Oh, you're a cop." A lot of people, even those in our communities, have the misconception in thinking that African American communities, and everyone in them, don't support the police. That's far from the truth. I'm on the phone on a regular basis with people from the community, from African American communities, that want to resolve the issues and the problems and get us past this whole "blue code of silence." And it's very difficult at times because you get it, there is a need. But there are times when officers are wholeheartedly targeted and where they're shot at. We just had something the other day where we had officers who were doing their job legitimately and had been targeted. I mean, I've lost friends on the department who have been killed in the line of duty for just doing their jobs and being good officers. There is a need across the country for better understanding on both sides. But it's very difficult as an African American because you see what's happening with the Black Lives Matter movement and you understand the need for it. It was a long time coming. But you also see the need where there has to be peaceful ways for us to go about protesting. And everyone is angry for a legitimate reason, because anytime someone is killed and it's not a justified incident, yeah . . . people should be angry. They should want to hold police officers accountable. It's understood. When officers and police departments aren't being transparent with these incidents, and things are happening where it looks like there's corruption, people have the right to protest us. That's in your First Amendment; you have the right to speak out about what's happening.

So, you see it as an African American officer. You support it to a point where it's peaceful and we're not doing the same things that some cops around the country have done to us, such as Walter Scott and Laquan McDonald. You have all these people . . . even the recent incidents in Baton Rouge . . . you have so many things happening where officers have taken someone's life and it's usually that same narrative. We know that more people are killed than just African Americans, but . . . that narrative . . . when you see it you are like, "Whoa, they're unarmed. And you see a video . . . they're shooting this person . . . they're running . . . there in a car . . . no one's in the direct line of getting killed . . . and cops are shooting at them. It makes you angry. As an African American cop, I understand both sides of it. As a cop, you know there have been times where I have been shot at. My partners have been shot at. I have friends who have been murdered in the line of duty for doing their jobs. You see both sides of it and sometimes you are in the middle, but the reality is that if all officers stood up and did things the right way, although we know they're going to make mistakes along the way because they're human. But, if we stood up and did things the right way, we would have more support. We would have people trust us more. I'm sorry it sounds like I'm rambling.

Terrell Carter: No, no, no. It sounds like you are answering multiple questions I planned on asking, so you knocked that out. But I did have two more questions for you on a personal level. We were going to get into a discussion about the Ethical Society. Your position with the Ethical Society and an explanation of that. Let me combine these last two personal questions. What do you wish people knew about your job, and what do you wish people knew about police officers as human beings?

Sergeant Taylor: I think the good majority of us come into this occupation with the grand idea of just being about helping and you're thinking about looking at it from the approach of helping people. And when we get here, we deal with so much, especially within [the] St. Louis Metropolitan Police Department. You get here and day to day, the internal stressors from your commanders, the demands of doing this and doing that, the lack of promotions, the lack of being able to get transfers when you're qualified, harsher disciplines for a lot of minorities on the department, and you know those things happen every day to someone you know. Not so much every day, but it happens so often . . . so frequently, and on top of that, you're going from call to call to call. One day you might get a call for a victim who has been raped and that victim may be eight years old. A week later you may get a call for a homicide and the victim may be an elderly female. You may get another call like something that just happened recently, and it was horrific, as well. A girl decided she wanted to stab a dog. You get all of these things happening, but during the course of your career, at the very beginning of your career is the only time you get that mental health assessment. That's where it's mandatory. It's when you start. It's not continuous over the course of your career unless someone like a commander forces you or another supervisor forces you. If people understood the lack of mental health screening and mental health welfare checks on officers . . . that's part of the problem with officers doing the things they shouldn't. It's not an excuse for bad behavior, but it's part of the problem. The lack of mental health, making it mandatory to receive screening, because sometimes you're [looked] upon as, "Awww, man, this officer just snapped." Really, most police departments can probably identify people, you know this, that you look at and think, "Man, I think that guy is going to snap one day." Most of the time they don't. All it takes is one officer with 16 rounds and two extra magazines to snap. And with the stresses of everyday work . . . you know.

Terrell Carter: Or with a baton or mace.

Sergeant Taylor: Mace . . . exactly. Everything you can name.

Terrell Carter: I have an acquaintance on the department who shot and killed someone. He got into a chase with a suspect and chased him into an area. It ended up the guy was much bigger than him. The guy went after his gun. He shot him. After the shooting he was sent downtown to headquarters for several weeks . . . months. . . . and I finally saw him at headquarters and I said, "Hey man. How are you doing?" He was like "fine." I was like, "Man, you shot and killed somebody. What do you mean you're doing fine?"

Sergeant Taylor: Exactly.

Terrell Carter: I asked, "What has the department done for you?" He said, "They gave me another bullet." That answers the question about what the department thinks. They didn't send him . . . they didn't mandate . . . they didn't require . . . They just said, "You . . . get off the street. You don't get to wear our uniform for a while."

Sergeant Taylor: A very little while.

Terrell Carter: Right. And we're going to give you a bullet to replace the one you used to kill someone else. So, obviously I agree wholeheartedly with what you just said. I'm going to say a couple of things to lead into the discussion on the Ethical Society. I am still acquaintances with multiple people on the department. And just a few moments ago you talked about the internal stressors on the department. About African Americans, minorities in general, because there are more minorities than just African Americans on the department, and them getting prized promotions or being transferred, or things like that. I ran into an officer who actually retired from the police department. He's a white gentleman and he did 25 years, or he worked 25 years. And I was like, "Hey, man. How are you doing? How is everything going on [in] the department? He said, "I had to retire. I had to get out of there." I asked him what was going on? What was wrong? He felt comfortable enough to say this to me, literally. "I wasn't going to get promoted. I wasn't black. I wasn't a woman. So, there was no way that I was going to have a real career on the department." I was like, "Wow, so what are you saying to me?" He said no one gets promoted on the police department unless they're black, a woman, or unless they're gay. I was like, "Well, that's not my experience, so I don't understand." He went on to say that there is a lot of tension from white officers, and again, this is a white man telling me this. He said that there was a lot of tension from white officers toward black officers . . . the same people that they worked with . . . because they felt like they were being left behind as second-class citizens (in order to promote blacks). But this occurred when we had our last (black) chief (Dan Isom), as well. And I'm not saying that it was true, or false, or whatever. Again, this was the narrative that was coming from him. Are you able to, I don't want to put you into a negative position, but can you address that? Is there tension between white officers and black officers . . . or is it. . . . There's a word that most people don't know about. It's called people with "steam." People with "steam" means that you are a person that works within the department that is connected to someone else who has some type of political capital or someone who can help you throughout your political. . . . Your career as a police officer. Whether it means that, if you're about to get into trouble, they can make a phone call and you don't get in trouble. If you want to get a prized transfer, as you talked about, you can get the transfer. If you want a promotion, you can get the promotion. Is it black against white? Is it people with steam versus people without steam? Is there a division on the department, or am I just hearing a story from just a grumpy old man?

Sergeant Taylor: Partly a grumpy old man, but you're absolutely right when it comes to any race. If you have anyone that's going to make a phone call for you, be it alderman, senator, judge, U.S. congressman/woman, anyone that's going to make a call on your behalf to someone high ranking within the police department, chances are you are going to have less discipline, but you're probably going to get promoted faster. The system is the cronyism, the biases, racism, sexism, all of those things exist. You know we're talking about human beings within the police department. Just as it happens everywhere else, we should hold ourselves to a higher standard. We don't in every situation. There is tension between African American officers and white officers. It exists. It does. You know, it's historically existed, but now, more so than ever, things are much worse. As far as African Americans go, I can speak directly from our perspective because I am African American, and over an association that's 97 percent African American. From our perspective, he's talking about who will not get promoted under Isom, but did you know that under Isom there were 13 sergeants, actually was it 15, who were eligible to be promoted. They were all white. So, if he's saying that happened under Chief Isom. . . . These officers were promoted under Dotson (a white chief who followed Isom). There are 16 (officers) eligible for promotion. He's (Dotson) promoted 14 of them. Correction. Fifteen of them. Fourteen white, one African American. When we talk about what he says, that unless you're black, that's absolutely far from the truth. You talk about, even under Isom who's African American, you had numbers like that. When you have a department [that is] 63 percent white, a mostly white male department, the jobs go to those that make up the majority. And we have 33.4 percent which are African American, yet the promotion numbers don't mirror those. It doesn't mirror that. From the rank of colonel, major, captain, and definitely not a lieutenant, where there are some outrageous number of lieutenants who are younger. There is going to be white, and mostly white male. So, when he says that, he's definitely misguided. It's unfortunate that he felt that way, but it's definitely not justified in his thinking. But we see things that are happening now with lawsuits, such as reverse discrimination lawsuits.

Terrell Carter: Like the lawsuit from (David) Bonenberger (a sergeant who won a lawsuit against the SLMPD for reverse discrimination when he was able to prove he was passed over for promotion due to his skin color).

Sergeant Taylor: Or like the lawsuit with Major Caruso which made the news. With Major Caruso, you have the things going on . . . I remember when I was an officer in South Patrol and he was over [at] the South Patrol (Detective) Bureau. There was already an African American female there, but they were trying to push me into the bureau. I had very little time on, so I shouldn't have been considered for the position. I didn't know what I was doing. When I asked him about me potentially being transferred back there when we already had an African American female, he essentially said, "You're not going to get back there." Not because I didn't have enough time on, which would have made more sense, but because I was black. You have people filing those kinds of lawsuits. There are all these stories that people don't get, and it's unfortunate because, if you think about the city and the (racial) division. . . . (For instance) we have two papers. We have a black paper (*St. Louis American*) and a predominantly white newspaper

(*Post-Dispatch*). Ninety-seven percent of the *Post-Dispatch* staff is white and at the *St. Louis American* there's a mixture (of races).

Terrell Carter: And the editor-in-chief of the black newspaper is a white male.

Sergeant Taylor: Exactly. And he's on top of it.

Terrell Carter: And he's a friend of mine, so I'm not saying it negatively.

Sergeant Taylor: He's a nice guy. But you know we have that, and then we have a black police officers union and a white police officers union. Correction. A black police officers association and a white police officers association within the police department. We are so divided, and everyone with their own opinions about what's going on, but the one thing that people can't get away from are the statistics. The statistics tell a different story.

Terrell Carter: Let's get into the statistics. But as we do that, tell everyone, tell our listeners what the Ethical Society of Police is. It's the African American society but explain a little more about it.

Sergeant Taylor: We're an African American police association that was founded in the 1960s by African Americans because racial discrimination came about. The focus and the goals are to bridge the gap between the community and the police department. That is our goal now. It has been our goal since I've become president. It was the goal when Eddie Simmons was president as well.

Terrell Carter: How long have you been president?

Sergeant Taylor: Since February of 2015.

Terrell Carter: Was this something you wanted to do? Was this something that you were the best person to . . . ?

Sergeant Taylor: I thought about it. I did it. I knew that I would probably be, and I'm not trying to be arrogant, probably be the best person for it. The former president, who we were so grateful for, has been indicted for stealing from the organization. He's a police officer. We wholeheartedly wanted him held accountable. We initiated the prosecution of the former president, Sergeant Darren Wilson. People have been. . . . We've received a little backlash from African Americans. "Well, you're putting another black man in jail." Well let me tell you.

Terrell Carter: He never should have done anything wrong. Period.

Sergeant Taylor: He committed a crime. Who cares if he's a police officer or not? He committed a crime. He needs to be held accountable. Just kind of forced . . . well sort of.

Terrell Carter: Why . . . you mention statistics . . . just a little background for our listeners, again. Recently, the Ethical Society conducted a study . . . released a study, and it was picked up by the *New York Times*. Would you mind talking about that because it talks about statistics, which you mentioned just a moment ago.

Sergeant Taylor: We felt the need to show the disparities, to show the cronyism, to show just . . . the issues within our police department as far as promotions . . . as far as transfers. You know about knowing someone (having steam) and having someone like you, and to get a job within the police department and in a specialized unit. And we have divisions within our police department that are about enforcement. These are the divisions that are about going out there and getting those crimes that are guns and dope and things like that and about that division being 80 percent white and mostly white male. You have over a 120-day time frame, 80 percent of people they arrested were African American, and we're not saying that a good majority of the people that they arrested didn't commit a crime because it's highly likely that they did. But when you add that into the racial profiling numbers for the last three years for this city of St Louis that show that African Americans are more likely to be stopped more but less likely to be found with contraband. That is for three years running that we stopped at. We did 2015, 2014, and 2013. I think we may have even done 2012 and it showed the same thing. So, you have these racial profiling numbers that tell a different story with contraband. Then you have these statistics within our police department that shows that . . . man . . . over 120 days, this unit that has mostly (mostly white males) . . . out of what, I think 11, one African American supervisor. You have these things that . . . on the surface they show that there is a problem. Or, if you think about how homicide . . . I believe right now, we're probably at 81 percent white for homicide (detectives). Ninety percent of the victims of homicides are African American. And this is traditionally, I think for the last four or five years. . . . So, you have this, and I'm not saying that these detectives and these division aren't capable of being just and fair; however, with solving crime, we go right back to the Department of Justice where it says that having diversity is critical to solving crime because you have people who can identify with people who are investigating their crimes. Or they feel comfortable with talking because you usually feel comfortable with people kind of like you. It's just a natural thing that happens. And we have this issue with outrageous crime, but we have some divisions that don't mirror . . . even slightly mirror that 33.4 percent demographic of African Americans within the police department. That's a problem. Other minorities are even worse. It's like 3 percent . . . 3 percent of our police department is Asian, Latino, and Hispanic. There is a lack of diversity, definitely.

Terrell Carter: Not that I'm going to stick to the report . . . there's the bigger question of how you get diversity on the police department . . . but let's finish talking about the report. The report was picked up obviously by multiple news stations in the St. Louis Metropolitan area. It made it all the way to New York, and it was a hot blip on the screen for just a second, and then something else occurred. What has been . . . how has this report, the stance of the Ethical Society doing that publicly . . . how has that [affected] the organization's ability to help its members . . . has it affected officers on an individual basis? Because, again, I know personally that when you stand up for something, and especially when you stand up for something that goes very high up or stand up against something that goes very high up, then you are going to have some type of retaliation. I'm not asking you to give specifics. Just in general, how has that affected the organization, and has it affected individual officers?

Sergeant Taylor: I can tell you we've had . . . one thing is that we have had tremendous support from the community and that's been our backbone. The community has been our rock, and they've held us accountable and wants us to stand up and do right. But internally, a good majority of our commanders are distant from us. You know there is that issue. When we bring up new issues that were in the report that have come to light, people are more forthcoming with us. They've reached out to us about different divisions in our police department where they're experiencing problems. At the airport . . . problems with the airport police. We have taken over (that force) with local control. Now we have these divisions where the airport . . . they have a major, a lieutenant, and a sergeant . . . they're all white. The airport (workforce) is probably about 60 percent African American. Then we have the deputy marshals. There you have mainly black and white officers with a white sergeant. We (Homicide) had a white sergeant, but now they're going to replace him because he's retired . . . and a white lieutenant. You're talking about seven people. One African American supervisor. Deputy marshals are mostly African American, so you have less taking over (leadership) of these divisions. Now, for the first time ever in the history of the city of St. Louis, there are a whole lot of issues that are coming to light. Mostly, we believe, because most of the time people cannot identify with people who are not like them, so it's just like the Department of Justice says when it comes to crime, it's important for those things to balance out. And to put qualified . . . we're not talking about putting unqualified African Americans in jobs. That's not what we want. But there needs to be a balance. So, problems are coming up. When we wrote the report, we didn't know about these issues. People now come forward. They feel comfortable. They're not going to stand for it. They're going to speak out, whether it's good, bad, or ugly. You know, we had to speak out about our former president. We want him to go to jail. So, we need to speak out about good things that are happening, and bad things, and people see that there's a balance. We have to also stand up for officers and police who have been targeted. Who have been killed in the line of duty. But we also have to speak out for people who have been targeted by police officers. Who have been murdered. Who have been unjustly charged with crimes, and things like that. People have begun to feel comfortable coming to us. A lot of people, on a daily basis, reach out to us to connect with us since then.

Terrell Carter: We've been talking for a while, and out of respect for your time, I want to ask you one last question. If you were given the opportunity to become a part of the leadership structure for the police department, what would be some of the first . . . or what would be some of the most crucial things that you would do . . . changes that you would make . . . things that you would implement?

Sergeant Taylor: The first thing that I would do would be . . . I know that in 2014 when Mike Brown was shot and killed by Darren Wilson, our police department came out, and we had some incidents as well here in the city where young men were shot and killed. But our chief and our command staff came out and said, "We are all about community engagement. This is what we're about, and this is how we're going to prove it. This is a priority." Well, you fast-forward two plus years later, there are three people assigned to community engagement. And the enforcement aspect of the police department, which is critical too, had a unit with 60 people. So, what is a priority? We're enforcing, and guess where it's getting us? We still have high crime. We're still not able to connect to get people to become informants. They don't feel comfortable enough with us to sign up to become informants. What I would do if I was in a command rank position? I would change our focus to community engagement because it will solve crimes. It will lower crimes, and on top of that, it will help you to connect. Another thing we do now is, we (Ethical Society) have a minority recruitment program. Actually, the recruitment program really isn't just for minorities. It's like everyone you know. We have Bosnian Americans. We have Russian Americans. We have Mexican Americans in our class. We have African Americans. We have whites. We have every race you can name. They have gone through our minority recruitment program. Essentially, what it does is, it's a pre-academy where we're more focused on morals and ethics. It's about bringing people in from the Black Lives Matter movement. People like the former chief of Ferguson, Missouri, Chief Dotson (the chief of St. Louis PD at the time of this recording). People that people may not like. People they may like. They tell them everything up-front. The good, the bad, and the ugly. That's what we focus on. It's about ethics. How to patrol. How to interact with people and talk to people. Positive things. Giving community service. It's that community engagement part again. That's what our class does. But, internally, guess what we face with that? Backlash from our chief, who now says that he's not really happy with the program despite the fact that, since October of 2015, we've had 30 people go through our minority recruitment program who have now become recruits in training as police officers. So, you know we have African American commanders, too, who are high-ranking captains and majors, but they're not really pleased with the program. But that's what I would do. I would focus on improving recruitment and building a new type of officer that's morally focused. That's about community engagement. I would make those things a priority. And it's not so much about having minorities as it is about having good people. You're going to get minorities that are great. You're going to get nonminorities that are great. If you make it more so focused on that and the mental health aspect of being a good officer, having a holistic approach, that's what our recruitment program is about. Those are the things I would focus on.

Postscript #3

WHAT CAN COMMUNITY PARTICIPATION LOOK LIKE?
A CASE STUDY

The Alliance for Interracial Dignity was founded in 2012 by leaders in the greater Webster Groves, Missouri, area. The hopes and dreams of the organization are stated in the following:

> Mission Statement: We, the Alliance, are bringing the community together by learning from our collective past, challenging the racial status quo, and building a stronger community.

> Vision: The Alliance for Interracial Dignity is committed to building a socially just community. The Alliance addresses issues of racial equity with the belief that making progress in this critical area will open the door to ending other forms of oppression.

> Core Belief: Equity requires that everyone has a voice and that diverse voices inform what our community looks and feels like across all aspects of life. This is particularly true of opportunities for civic leadership, employment, education, housing, entertainment, and recreation. (Dignity 2018)

The following is a document titled *Prop P: Community Conversation Report* that the alliance produced as a part of the process to negotiate with the city of Webster Groves, Missouri, how a recently approved tax increase would be best utilized by the city for improved relationships between citizens and law enforcement.

Public Safety: A Community Conversation

Background

On January 24, 2018, the Alliance for Interracial Dignity partnered with the City of Webster Groves to host a "Community Conversation" about public safety. The impetus for the meeting was the recent passage of Proposition P, a St. Louis County ballot measure which, to quote the measure, *"impose[s] a one-half of one percent sales tax for the purpose of providing funds to improve police and public safety in St. Louis County and each of the municipalities within St. Louis County."* Webster Groves now receives about $1.15 million annually in Prop P funds.

The ballot language is very broad, and several media sources reported confusion in various areas of the county about how Prop P money is to be used. To respond to that confusion and ensure spending would be in keeping with the intent of the Prop P campaign promises, the St. Louis County Council issued a resolution asking elected officials in municipalities to use the money in a manner consistent with voters' intent. A portion of that reads: *"Cognizant that each municipality receiving Prop P tax revenue will have to make its own decisions within the meaning of the Prop P ballot language, the County Council urges all elected municipal officials to approach the issue mindful of the will of the people whose money will be used, as expressed by the vote on Prop P, and to join with St. Louis County in making their decisions transparently, openly, and with the meaningful involvement of the people they represent."*

It is the mission of the Alliance to bring people together to learn from our collective past, challenge the racial status quo, and build a stronger community. The Alliance saw this as an important opportunity to bring the community together to build our collective muscle and ability to dialogue constructively and openly about policing and public safety—including budget priorities—in coming years.

The Community Conversation

Over 50 people participated in the Community Conversation, including numerous community members, Mayor Gerry Welch, Chief of Police Dale Curtis, Captain Stephen Spear, several members of City Council and the School Board, and several candidates in the upcoming local election. Although the Alliance organized this forum with city officials from Webster Groves, neighboring municipalities were informed of our hope to ultimately involve them in a regional conversation. Community members participated from Webster, Shrewsbury, Rock Hill, and beyond.

Much of the meeting was spent in eight small groups of six to eight members each, with the guiding questions: *What expectations do you have for greater public safety and stronger police-community support for one another? How might you expect to see these values expressed in our city budget?* Each group kept notes and reported out three main ideas to the meeting at-large. (See addendum for complete notes.) Chief Curtis and Captain Spear then had an opportunity to respond and report current police department initiatives. Meeting participants also stayed for an impromptu question and answer session with Chief Curtis that went almost half an hour past the allotted time.

Participants at the meeting had an opportunity to complete a paper survey indicating their spending priorities for Proposition P funds. This same survey was also circulated online and at several community meetings, including a sampling of PTO meetings, the North Webster Neighborhood Coalition monthly meeting, and the school district's Equity in Education Committee meeting. This resulted in a total of 102 responses to the survey.

This report compiles and synthesizes the results of the survey with the notes from the Community Conversation and makes recommendations for next steps as suggested by the process results.

Community Response

Participants demonstrated an active interest in learning about, and contributing to, the strategic planning process of the police department. The overarching priorities identified from this community conversation include: training, police/citizen interaction, accountability, and transparency.

Overwhelmingly, conversation participants expressed a strong desire to see funds dedicated to ongoing, high quality anti-bias and de-escalation training. Additionally, they want more information about what that training includes, as well as to see metrics that measure officers' progress in the areas of anti-bias and de-escalation training. One group would like to see progress tied to an Annual Performance Review, and also shared particular interest and concern about training for school resource officers working with children. Overall, citizens wanted to know specifically what training is being implemented and to be able to see the measure of its effectiveness. Some expressed interest in local officers' training with other departments to exchange best practices regionally.

Frequently discussed was the desire for more interaction and community engagement. Participants would like to see a robust budget for meaningful community engagement that builds trust, and two groups specifically mentioned adding a community liaison position. Participants noted that even though the department publishes information and makes officers available at community events, more outreach is needed to understand why citizen participation with these efforts is often very low. Also, key in several groups' commentaries was a desire to see more evidence of a community policing model. Four groups noted hopes to enhance programming and services that reach youth. Two groups requested a substation in North Webster, noting the desire to enhance the community policing model along with that proposed substation. Some participants expressed concern about racial bias and how that bias manifests in the experiences of police and citizens.

Accountability and transparency were heartfelt sentiments amongst all groups. Four groups requested a civilian advisory board, and two groups specifically requested body cameras. There were also suggestions to make a specific line in the city budget for Prop P monies.

Citizens expressed support for the police department, and perception of the department among participants appears to be generally positive. Nonetheless, participants requested more accessible touch points that would allow citizens to measure and quantify the efficacy of their public investment in the department.

Survey Response

The survey is based on a combination of suggestions raised at prior Alliance meetings, Prop P surveys used in other municipalities, and the police reform "Calls to Action" in the Forward Through Ferguson report. Respondents could indicate a preference to defer to the priorities of police and fire officials, and there was also room for respondents to write in their own suggestions.

The Alliance received 102 completed surveys. It is interesting to note that the group discussions mirrored almost exactly what community members expressed on the survey. (See addendum for survey and complete results.) While 27 surveys were completed by individuals on the night of the community conversation, 75 came from citizens outside of that event.

Table 1   Summary of Survey Responses

De-escalation training	77
Anti-bias training	72
Wellness services	59
Youth programming	57
Body and dash cams	49
Civilian Review Board	48
Protest response plan	30
Raise salaries	22
Establish substation(s)	16
Hire additional officers	14
Defer to police priorities	9

"Please check the uses you think are most important for Prop P funds."

Next Steps

These are the recommendations for next steps as suggested by the results and outcomes of this specific process.

1. The city council, police department, and citizens should work together to create sustainable parameters to develop a Citizen Advisory Board. The nomination and selection process for the citizen advisors should be completely transparent and benefit from the guidance of those parameters created. Once established, that Citizen Advisory Board could provide feedback for the development of community engagement programming, mechanisms for citizen input, and increased measures of accountability and transparency.

2. Provide a detailed report of Prop P expenditures on a yearly basis.

3. Conduct a review of the anti-bias and de-escalation training currently in place; search for other evidence based, research informed programs for purposes of comparison; seek professional feedback on the programming; and determine a metric to show departmental growth as a result of that training.

4. Consider hiring a community liaison or community engagement officer, and also increasing the budget for meaningful and robust community engagement programs.

5. Consider the development of a substation in North Webster.

6. Allocate resources to the study of effective community policing programs nationwide and implement those best practices in Webster

Groves. The term "community policing" was widely and regularly used by many citizens during this conversation. Further information is needed regarding citizens' perceptions and expectations surrounding the idea of what the term "community policing" encompasses.

7. Plan continuations of the community conversation about public safety at regular intervals.

8. Interface with Rock Hill and Shrewsbury to share this process and the results. Consider a joint effort for a multi-community conversation in the future.

Support from the Alliance for Interracial Dignity

The Alliance for Interracial Dignity is committed to assisting the city of Webster Groves with the steps listed above, including but not limited to the establishment of a Citizens Advisory Board (or similar organization) and assistance with the organization and facilitation of future community conversations and community engagement opportunities. The Alliance sees the results of this forum and partnership with the city of Webster Groves as an opportunity to collaborate to bring citizens together to build a stronger community in which each and every person feels emotionally and physically safe, experiences a strong sense of belonging, and feels valued in their community.

Addendum

Pages 7–14 are the verbatim written notes collected from the various small groups at the community conversation. Each small group recorded general notes of their discussion, then created a poster highlighting three main goals to present to the large group of all participants.

Pages 15–17 show the survey circulated at community meetings and online via the Alliance for Interracial Dignity, Webster Groves Community Connect, and Webster Groves Alternative Community Facebook forums; provide exact survey results; and list the verbatim verbiage of the individual surveys' "other" response lines.

The Community Conversation: Group Discussion Notes

Group 1

Poster

- De-escalation training
  - Repeated periodically

- Civilian Review Board
    - Systematic review of responsibilities of police policy
    - Respond to individual complaints
- 2nd Police Substation
    - In North Webster (Douglass Manor?)

Table Notes

- Police Issues:
    - Break-ins to unlocked cars
    - Car-jacking
    - North Webster/Ivory Crockett Park: "Drug activity, hanging out"
    - People dressed like utility workers/rumors of break-ins
- Statistics on police stops reflect that more black people are getting stopped
    - People tell their pastor they feel bias exists against people of color
    - Police: profiling-by-proxy: neighbors report things based on bias
- Ideas:
    - De-escalation training
    - Data collection on police stops (publicly available)
    - Civilian review board: systemic as well as individual response
    - Defer to priorities of police/fire
    - 2nd police substation in North Webster

Group 2

Poster

- Training
    - Anti-bias training
    - Call center response
    - De-escalation training
- Community Policing:
    - Interacting with the neighborhood
    - Building trust
    - Youth programming

- Body cameras/benefit from body cameras
  - Increased self-consciousness
  - Police behave better
  - Difficulties are reduced

Table Notes

- Training
  - Anti-bias training
- Reasonable pay—we are attracting workers
- Community policing
  - Interacting with the community, in the part, around, not in their cars
  - "The more you get to know people, the more connections they can establish to move Information out of people"
  - Developing a trust with the neighborhood
- Body Cameras
  - Difficulties are reduced
  - Police behave better
- Centralized call center, improve dispatch service

Group 3

Poster

- Substation in North Webster with the focus on community policing
- Mandate annual training
  - anti-bias and de-escalation/mental health services for first responders
- Police Advisory/Review Board

Table Notes

- Community policing/foot patrols is an area of need
  - Perhaps with emphasis in warmer months when people congregate
- Substations in areas of need (North Webster?)
  - These substations should have a focus on community policing policies
- Mandatory annual training for anti-bias and de-escalating situations
- Possibly a police advisory board to share experiences and concerns

- Evaluate the need for mental health services for first responders (access for services)
  - Postcards for citizens that might need services for different afflictions

Group 4

Poster

- Information Sharing
  - Prior to crimes/patterns—where is the info?
  - What happens post-crime/investigation?
  - How many crimes solved/unsolved?
  - Public safety concerns of officers?
  - Why do people want to be cops in Webster?
- Community Policing—Beat Cops
- De-escalation
  - Best techniques
  - Anti-bias training (covered in hiring process?)
  - Mental health training/assessment

Table Notes

- Attempted robbery of Dewey's delivery at 2am
  - Worried about repetition
  - Is this a real depiction of Webster?
- Hear from police more often; not just coffee with a cop
  - See statistics
  - What's the follow up?
- Why do cops come to Webster to work?
  - We don't have much crime
- North Webster
  - More feedback from North Webster is desired
  - How do police address issues?
  - Racial profiling in Webster
- De-escalation and Anti-bias training; dashboard/cameras
  - Do body cameras actually produce results?
  - Mental health screening?

Group 5

Poster

- Prop P earmarked for specified field?
  - i.e. police, fire?
- Racial bias training
  - We want it to be cutting edge
- Mental health checks/services for officer care
- Building trust between officers/kids/community
- Traffic and Pedestrian Safety
  - Designated crosswalks and sidewalks for walking to school

Table Notes

- Will Prop P funds be earmarked for any certain fields?
- Racial bias training that is cutting edge
- Mental health checks for officers and counseling
- Building trust with officers and increased training
- Traffic safety: adding stop signs and crosswalks

Group 6

Poster

- Enable residents to get to know their neighbors (better)
- A stronger police and community relationship
  - Community Liaison?
  - Elementary school engagement
- Investing in Public/Community Spaces
  - access/ownership
  - Youth
  - Sidewalks

Table Notes

- People get to know their neighbors better
- A police relationship with the community
  - Sharing viewpoints and understanding

- Hear and see more of the community members
- Community liaison
- Investing in public/community spaces

Group 7

Poster

- More Knowledge
  - What are public safety concerns to officers?
  - How are funds spent now?
  - What/how are services coordinated?
- Strategic Planning Process
  - Long term 3, 5-year plans
  - Community input on what is "safety" and fund allocation in response
- Transparent/Collaborative
  - Line Item for Prop P
    - Public approval/allow time for comments
  - Specify how services are collaborative and saving us money while making us safer

Table Notes

- What are the department's safety issues?
- Retention of police force—initial reason for Prop P
- Greater collaboration between departments, more public-facing interaction/cooperation
  - Break down silos, share best practices, public-facing collaboration is a crime deterrent
- Transparent, public-accounting of total Prop P $1.15 million
- Who determines expenditure?
  - Police bring budget to committee for approval?
- Defining public safety: roads, school routes:
  - 3-year goal? 5-year goal?
- Not a clear definition or understanding of what issues we face re: police department
- We need program design information, knowing basic info; what are the department's main issues?

- Broad community based strategic planning process
- Comment period on budget
- Shared professional development between sister departments

Group 8

Poster

- Transparency
  - Body cameras
  - Who reviews complaints? What is that process?
  - Tools for public to see and measure effects of anti-bias training
- Citizen Review Board or Advisory Board
  - A way to be transparent
  - Would knowing there is public oversight and involvement in complaint and resolution process affect who feels comfortable making a complaint?
- Community Engagement
  - Dedicate more of the budget for this
  - Have a top down model of community engagement that builds trust
  - Measure and report out officer community engagement hours that are non-confrontational interaction hours

Table Notes

- Transparency
  - Body cameras and dash cameras can help but we have to have good policy that goes along with that to support police officer professionalism and professional discretion in how they choose to interact and make decisions/whether or not to arrest
  - Training should be ongoing/part of publicly available Annual Performance Review
- Community Engagement that has a robust budget
  - Top down model of community engagement that builds trust
  - Require, and also require transparent-reporting-out of officer community engagement hours that are non-confrontational interaction
- Transparent tools to see and measure the progress the police department is making in anti-bias training, de-escalation training, lessening of racial profiling (data supported)

- Question about use of force policy: how is it rated? Where is the transparency in that? Would a citizen review board or citizen advisory board be a good idea? Who currently hears and reviews complaints? How does that affect whether or not people feel safe making complaints?
- SCHOOL RESOURCE OFFICERS:
  - Are they under the control of the police department or school district? Who pays them?
  - What is the training for being a school resource officer? Do they get special training on how to work with teenagers?
  - Do they get special training to work with kids who might have special needs or behavioral issues?

After the table sessions, the Alliance conducted a survey among community members (the Webster Groves Proposition P Survey, Winter 2017–18) to see how they thought that the funds should be allocated. While the survey itself suggested some potential responses (such as "purchase body and dashboard cameras" and "hire additional officers") it also included an "other" section where community meeting participants could write in their own suggestions. Many community members utilized the "other" option, suggesting that the funds be used to "create a civilian partnership board with the police," "invest in public spaces and infrastructure," and staff increased patrols around local neighborhoods, among other initiatives. Due to the buy-in of the community, the collaborative and inclusive nature of the process, and the willingness of city leaders to actively engage in the process, a final plan is being developed from the accumulated data with plans for future implementation.

Postscript #4

DO THEY BELONG HERE?

Galatians 3:21–29
(Unpublished Sermon: June 19, 2016)

One of the most iconic human characters from the children's television show *Sesame Street* is Susan Robinson. Susan is a nurse who lives in the Sesame Street neighborhood and is married to Gordon Robinson, a school teacher. Quick trivia fact: Susan is one of the four longest-running original characters from the *Sesame Street* series. The other three longest-running characters are Bob, Big Bird, and Oscar the Grouch, who are both voiced by the same person. The other longest-running character is Kermit the Frog, originally voiced by *Sesame Street* and *Muppet Show* creator Jim Henson.

The actress who plays Susan is Loretta Mae Long, who got her first big break in acting during the 1960s through *Sesame Street.* One of the reasons that Mrs. Long continues to act on *Sesame Street* is because she is a staunch believer in education. So much so that she actually earned a PhD during the early years of *Sesame Street.* Her dissertation was titled "Sesame Street: A Space Age Approach to Education for Space Age Kids." It examined the educational model used on *Sesame Street* and its effects on children.

One of my favorite skits of the show was the song "One of These Things Is Not Like the Others." I really enjoyed watching her and Kermit perform it together. It involved two characters looking at a screen that contained three to four objects. Two or three of the objects would be similar, while one would be wholly different. The words of the song reflected this. In its original incarnation, the words were, "One of these things is not like the others. One of these things just doesn't belong. Can you tell which thing is not like the others by the time I finish my song?" The other character(s) would then follow up by saying, "Did you guess which thing was not like the others? Did you guess which thing just doesn't belong? If you guessed this one is not like the others, then you're absolutely . . . right!"

Another version of the song went, "Three of these things belong together. Three of these things are kind of the same. Can you guess which one of these doesn't belong here? Now it's time to play our game." In the 1980s, the lyrics changed to, "Three of these kids belong together. Three of these kids are kind of the same. But one of these kids is doing his (her) own thing. Now it's time to play our game. It's time to play our game."

What was the purpose of the song and video segment? It was to help children get into the habit of understanding and identifying what made something in a group different from the other things in that group. Whether it was differences based on shape, color, material, or even its intended use/ purpose. Shoes would be grouped together versus a lone shirt. Circles would be grouped together contrasted against a single square. Items that were red would be grouped together against a single blue item. The "One of These Things" segments started out with simple examples like this, but over the years, the segments became more complicated in order to challenge children to identify more complex patterns, such as understanding which tools could be used to drive a nail or turn a screw into wood.

Like many kids that watched *Sesame Street* religiously, I learned how to recognize similar patterns based on a wide variety of criteria. These kinds of skills aren't just good for kids to learn so they can put toys in the correct boxes or know which blocks go together. Learning how to do this, recognize patterns of similarity, can become something valuable that we are all able to use in life. For example, I used the skills that I learned in recognizing patterns and similarities when I worked as a carpenter's apprentice and carpenter. I was able to read blueprints and recognize patterns for how a wall, or entire floor, was designed and to be laid out. The ability to see similar things and recognize patterns became a good skill to have.

On the flip side, I think that children and grownups learn how to do something else through these types of *Sesame Street* exercises. I think the skills that are learned through exercises like the "One of These Things" idea also teach people how to quickly identify things that are different. It teaches children how to quickly identify something that's out of place. Something that may not belong where it is because of what makes it different from the other items being examined. Instead of seeing what looks alike first, you learn how to see what's different first. You are able to identify what sticks out as unique. That skill can also be very valuable in life.

When I was a police officer patrolling the streets of St. Louis, I learned how to use the skill of identifying something that was different, something that was out of place, something that didn't belong where it was, in order to help fight crime and to try to make other people's lives better.

Whether a person is a police officer or simply a mother who's examining a child after a day playing at the park, there is great value in being able to see something and quickly tell if it's in the right place or not.

You may now be thinking, "Okay, Terrell. Thanks for the trip down memory lane. Thanks for making sure that goofy song is now stuck in our minds. Please tell us what any of this has to do with the Bible passage from Galatians 3:21–29. Being able to identify the things that belong together in a certain setting or context is a valuable skill that we all can, and probably already have, cultivated. But, let me ask this question. Is there ever a time when that skill can become a not-so-good thing? Is there ever a time when it can become detrimental? My answer to this goofy question is "yes."

I say "yes" because at its simplest level, the Book of Galatians is dealing with the ideas of similarity and uniqueness and how we can respond to them. It is dealing with how the early church worked through the idea of "one of these things doesn't belong here." One of Paul's goals in writing this letter is to deal with the question of "Which of these things doesn't belong here and which of these things does" and, ultimately, what the Church's response to it should be.

As I have pointed out over the past few Sundays, the main question that Paul was dealing with in the letter was whether non-Jews, with all of their uniqueness and differences from people that followed traditional Judaism like Jesus and the 12 disciples, whether these Gentiles could and should be counted as equal members in the family of God. Could a group of people who were different from Jesus' lineage and the lineage of the people that were closest to him, who didn't follow the same rules as Jesus and the people that followed him while he was alive, could these types of people be fully incorporated into God's family, just as they were?

From the passages that we've explored over the past few weeks, we learned that Paul thought that the answer was "yes," but some of the disciples that previously walked with Jesus weren't fully convinced of this. In prior verses, Paul reflected on how Peter, one of Jesus' original followers, was okay with non-Jews being seen as equals, as long as his more conservative friends from Jerusalem weren't around. As long as it was just him and Paul spending time with non-Jews, Peter was okay with eating with them and spending quality time with them. But as soon as more conservative Jewish people came around, he stopped spending time with the non-Jews and stopped eating with them.

Paul called Peter on the carpet for this. Paul told Peter that, essentially, he was being two-faced because he let his fear of what someone else thought cause him to change his actions toward people that simply wanted to be included in God's family. In Galatians 3:21–29, Paul stressed to his readers that they don't have to try to be like the disciples, or anyone else, who has the same racial or cultural lineage as Jesus in order to be pleasing to God. Following the law shouldn't be their focus, because following the law couldn't make a person acceptable before God.

Today, instead of quoting a bunch of people who are smarter than me in order to make my point, I want to simply read Paul's words and interact with them in order to let them stand for themselves. I will read Paul's words from The Message version of the Bible.

In verses 21 and 22, Paul suggests that the law was a tool that God used in order for people to be drawn closer to the "Holy." Paul says, "Is the law, then, an anti-promise, a negation of God's will for us? Not at all. Its purpose was to make obvious to everyone that we are, in ourselves, out of right relationship with God, and therefore to show us the futility of devising some religious system for getting by our own efforts what we can only get by waiting in faith for God to complete his promise. For if any kind of rule-keeping had power to create life in us, we would certainly have gotten it by this time."

Through these words, Paul suggests that if rules could've made us right with God, then those who had made it their life's mission to follow those rules would have already been perfect. There wouldn't have been a need for a Savior to come and die in the first place. But that wasn't the case. Following rules didn't justify anyone.

He says in verses 23–24 that the law was a tool to help people focus on God until they could understand what was available to them through faith. He says, "Until the time when we were mature enough to respond freely in faith to the living God, we were carefully surrounded and protected by the Mosaic Law. The law was like those Greek tutors, with which you are familiar, who escort children to school and protect them from danger or distraction, making sure the children will really get to the place they set out for."

Paul implies that the law was only a temporary tool that had a specific place in life [or] a specific purpose. It was to be like a guide that directed people as they walked through [or] journeyed through the process of learning more about God and God's desires. The word that Paul uses is "pedagogue" or custodian. A pedagogue wasn't a teacher. He or she was a slave that led children to and from school during the time period that Paul lived. Their job was to make sure that the master's children made it to and from school every day.

The law was with them, protecting and guiding them until they could comprehend God's bigger plan and purpose of restoration and relationship for all as found in Christ. And now that the bigger purpose and plan had been revealed, they no longer had to depend on the law. Paul says, "But now you have arrived at your destination: By faith in Christ you are in direct relationship with God. Your baptism in Christ was not just washing you up for a fresh start. It also involved dressing you in an adult faith wardrobe—Christ's life, the fulfillment of God's original promise."

If I'm understanding Paul's words correctly, he's saying that following the law is not what changes a person. Following the law only shows you what you can't do, or what you can't get right on your own. Following the law shows you where you are weak and what you are incapable of accomplishing on your own. Following God is what changes you. Making Christ your focus, following his life example and teachings, is what changes you. That is what causes you to become a new person that is acceptable to God. This was God's intent from the very beginning. Not to follow rules, but to follow God's Son. God doesn't require a person to follow a set of rules or to adopt a restrictive lifestyle in order to be happy with you. Christ's imprint on your life is what pleases God.

I know that I said that I wouldn't quote multiple authors today, but I do want to share the words of Dr. Robert A. Bryant because I believe they are a relevant clarification of Paul's thoughts. Dr. Bryant says, "What, then, shall one make of Paul's curious critique of the law? According to Paul, God gave the law 'because of transgressions.' The law exposed selfishness and self-righteousness—sin and idolatry of every sort. It uncovered rebelliousness against God's will. The law did not have the power, however, to make people holy. It was not a remedy for sin; its work was diagnostic. It could be obeyed, but it did not seal within hearts a love for God and neighbor. Thus, Paul says that the law served as a tutor, a gift from God to guide the people of Israel until they came of age to receive their full inheritance when Christ came. The law was given to prepare Israel for Christ's coming."

Paul goes on to say, "In Christ's family there can be no division into Jew and non-Jew, slave and free, male and female. Among us you are all equal.

That is, we are all in a common relationship with Jesus Christ. Also, since you are Christ's family, then you are Abraham's famous 'descendant,' heirs according to the covenant promises."

Dr. Bryant adds to Paul's words by saying, "The true heirs of Abraham, then, are not those who keep the law but those who follow Christ, the 'seed' of Abraham. Moreover, Paul insists that the promise of God to Abraham and Abraham's trust in God preceded the law and are, therefore, better than trust in the law. If one belongs to Christ, then, one must be a 'seed' of Abraham whose life and relationships will be governed by the Lord's Spirit, which is available in this new era to Gentiles and Jews alike. All of God's children may now relate to God directly through the Spirit of (God's) Son rather than through the tutor called 'law.' God has ended the law's work as a tutor, because the age of faith has now come."

In Christ, they were all free to be themselves and to still be confident that God was with them, regardless of external criteria. God didn't restrict God's love for people to one racial or cultural group or only to people that followed a set of rules or who viewed life in one particular way. Access to God and God's love was open to everyone who was willing to accept it. I wish that everyone saw things this way.

Okay, Terrell. Are you saying that God doesn't have a standard that we are held to? No, I'm not saying that. There is clearly a standard that we all are held to. That standard isn't a set of rules that simply show us how bad we are and how we all fail to measure up to God's best wishes. Our standard is Jesus, who was the fulfillment of the law and all of the rules that were given in the first place. Okay, Terrell, that's nice. We've heard you say that before. But wasn't the law and the 10 Commandments the standard that Jesus lived by? Yes, but he also transcended those things when he was asked by someone what the most important law there was that needed to be followed.

You all remember his response, don't you? He said that all of the laws and the commandments were summed up in two rules. Love God. Love others. That is how you fulfill the law. Let me also continue to clarify that Paul wasn't against the law. We just read his words saying that the law served a purpose. But I think that Paul was concerned about how the law and its application were being used to keep people at odds with each other.

Like Paul, I'm not against rules or traditions. But I do have concerns that are similar to Paul's. I'm concerned about our human tendencies to use laws and rules as a way to make sure that people are the same, or as similar to us as possible. I'm concerned about our human tendencies to use laws and rules as a way to keep things from changing and losing our personal power or influence. I'm concerned about our human tendencies to use rules and regulations to keep the focus on fulfilling our personal desires and preferences.

I'm concerned about our human tendency to use law and rules to punish people who may be different from us or have different life experiences.

We see this play out in so many arenas of our country and culture. Whether it's during an election cycle where we see people attempting to control the rules in order to serve their own self-interests and keep things the same as they have been. Or whether we see this take place in churches where people try to categorize people so they can be pigeonholed into a particular group.

Dr. Elisabeth Johnson, pastor of a prominent Lutheran church, tells the story of overhearing one of her female congregation members being doggedly questioned by another member on a particular issue. The person was trying to find out whether this woman was "conservative" or "liberal," so they could know how to classify her in the future. The female member, who refused to accept either label, finally answered, "I am a child of God and that's what matters." The person asking all the questions left in a huff.

Dr. Johnson said that this made her realize something. "Our continued attempts to categorize and label one another in the church, and to (divide ourselves and to) diminish one another on the basis of those categories and labels, are signs of our spiritual immaturity. Paul reminds us that since Christ has come, we are no longer enslaved to old divisions. All are justified solely by what God has done for us by one we believe is more powerful than us. Through baptism into Christ, we belong to him and to one another. All share fully and equally in the inheritance of God's promises and in the mission to which God has called us."

For this assurance, we can give God praise. Amen.

STUDIES FOR FURTHER CONSIDERATION

The following are summaries of quantitative studies that have been produced within the past eight years by academics, community groups, and governmental agencies, as well as court cases that have identified grossly unjust police practices. These studies, on their own and combined, show a consistent experience for blacks as it relates to experiencing unnecessary levels of force from police even though they were not exhibiting actions that necessarily warranted that police force.

- A study by a University of California, Davis, professor found "evidence of a significant bias in the killing of unarmed black Americans relative to unarmed white Americans, in that the probability of being black, unarmed, and shot by police is about 3.49 times the probability of being white, unarmed, and shot by police on average."

- An independent analysis of *Washington Post* data on police killings found that "when factoring in threat level, black Americans who are fatally shot by police are, in fact, less likely to be posing an imminent lethal threat to the officers at the moment they are killed than white Americans fatally shot by police."

- An analysis of the use of lethal force by police in 2015 found no correlation between the level of violent crime in an area and that area's police killing rates. That finding, by the Black Lives Matter–affiliated group Mapping Police Violence, disputes the idea that police only kill people when operating under intense conditions in high-crime areas. Mapping Police Violence found that fewer than one in three black people killed by police in 2016 were suspected of a violent crime or armed.

- The Department of Justice's investigation into the behavior of police in Ferguson, Missouri, found "a pattern or practice of unlawful conduct within the Ferguson Police Department that violates the First, Fourth, and Fourteenth Amendments to the United States Constitution, and federal statutory law." The scathing report found that the department was targeting black residents and treating them as revenue streams for the city by striving to continually increase the money brought in through fees and fines. "Officers expect and demand compliance even when they lack legal authority," the report's authors wrote. "They are inclined to interpret the exercise of free-speech rights as unlawful disobedience, innocent movements as physical threats, indications of mental or physical illness as belligerence." (Makarechi 2016)

These summaries also show the disparity between how often blacks are stopped by police, whether they are walking or driving, because police think they are good prospects for a drug or contraband arrest.

- A 2014 analysis of Illinois Department of Transportation data by the American Civil Liberties Union found the following: "African American and Latino drivers are nearly twice as likely as white drivers to be asked during a routine traffic stop for 'consent' to have their car searched. Yet white motorists are 49% more likely than African American motorists to have contraband discovered during a consent search by law enforcement, and 56% more likely when compared to Latinos."

- A 2013 ruling by a New York Federal District Court judge found that the New York Police Department's "stop and frisk" practices violated the constitutional rights of minority citizens of the city. Between January 2004 and June 2012, the city conducted 4.4 million stops. Eighty-eight percent of those stops resulted in no further action, and 83 percent of the stopped population were black or Hispanic, despite the fact that those minority groups, together, made up just over half of the city's overall population. (Makarechi 2016)

Finally, these summaries evidence the fact that being black is associated with being a criminal, even when that black person is actually a law enforcement official.

- A 2016 study by a team of professors from UCLA, Harvard, Portland State University, and Boston University analyzed suspects' booking photographs for phenotypical signs of whiteness to test the following hypothesis: "the Whiter one appears, the more the suspect will be protected from police force." Their findings: "police used less force with highly stereotypical Whites, and this protective effect was stronger than the effect for non-Whites."

- A 2010 governor's task force examining police-on-police shootings found even black and Latino police officers face a greater risk of being killed by police. In cases of mistaken identity, 9 out of the 10 off-duty officers killed by other officers in the United States since 1982 were black or Latino. (Makarechi 2016)

Bibliography

Alliance for Interracial Dignity. *Homepage.* May 1, 2018. Accessed May 1, 2018. http://allianceforinterracialdignity.org/.

Anderson, Elijah. "Race, Space, Integration, and Inclusion?: The White Space." *Sociology of Race and Ethnicity* 1, no. 1 (2015): 10–21.

Balko, Radley. *Five Myths about America's Police.* December 18, 2014. Accessed July 24, 2018. https://www.washingtonpost.com/opinions /five-myths-about-americas-police/2014/12/05/35b1af44-7bcd -11e4-9a27-6fdbc612bff8_story.html?utm_term=.c6926761fc8f.

Bulck, Jan J. M. Van Den. "Fictional Cops: Who Are They, and What Are They Teaching Us?" In *Law Enforcement, Communication, and Community,* edited by Howard Giles, 107–27. Philadelphia: John Benjamins Publishing, 2002.

Carter, Terrell. *Healing Racial Divides: Finding Strength in Our Diversity.* St. Louis: Chalice Press, 2019.

Carter, Terrell. *Walking the Blue Line: A Police Officer Turned Community Activist Provides Solutions to the Racial Divide.* San Diego: Bettie Youngs Books, 2015.

Chambliss, William J. *Power, Politics, and Crime.* New York: Routledge, 2018.

Cleland, Skylar. *Why Police Officers Are the Silent Heroes of America.* January 30, 2017. Accessed June 7, 2018. https://www.theodysseyonline .com/police-officers-everyday-heroes.

Cone, James H. "Theology's Great Sin: Silence in the Face of White Supremacy." In *The Cambridge Companion to Black Theology,* edited by Dwight Hopkins and Edward P. Antonio, 344. New York: Cambridge University Press, 2012.

Craven, Julia. *National Police Group Apologizes for Past Racial Injustices, But Not Current Ones.* October 18, 2016. Accessed October 18, 2016. https://www.huffingtonpost.com/entry/iacp-police-racism-apology _us_58054347e4b0b994d4c0f326.

Eberhardt, Jennifer L., Paul G. Davies, Valerie J. Purdie-Vaughns, and Sheri Lynn Johnson. "Looking Deathworthy: Perceived Stereotypicality of Black Defendants Predicts Capital-Sentencing Outcomes." *Psychological Science* 17, no. 5 (2006): 383–86.

Eberhardt, Jennifer L., Phillip Atiba Goff, Valerie J. Purdie, and Paul G. Davies. "Seeing Black: Race, Crime, and Visual Processing." *Journal of Personality and Social Psychology* 87, no. 6 (2004): 876–93.

Editorial Board. "Don't Shoot." *The Christian Century* December 3 (2014): 7.

Escobar, Edward J. *Race, Police, and the Making of a Political Identity: Mexican Americans and the Los Angeles Police Department, 1900–1945.* Berkeley: University of California Press, 1999.

Free, Marvin D. *Racial Issues in Criminal Justice: The Case of African Americans.* Santa Barbara: Greenwood Publishing, 2003.

Frisby, Cynthia M. "Misrepresentations of Lone Shooters: The Disparate Treatment of Muslim, African-American, Hispanic, Asian, and White Perpetrators in the U.S. News Media." *Advances in Journalism and Communication*, 5, no. 2 (2017): 162–81.

Frizzell, Laura, Sadé L. Lindsay, and Scott Duxbury. *Media Coverage More Empathetic for Mass Shooters Who Are White: Study.* July 29, 2018. Accessed July 30, 2018. https://faithfullymagazine.com/media-cove rage-more-empathetic-for-mass-shooters-who-are-white-study/.

Goff, Phillip Atiba, Jennifer L. Eberhardt, Melissa J. Williams, and Matthew Christian Jackson. "Not Yet Human: Implicit Knowledge, Historical Dehumanization, and Contemporary Consequences." *Journal of Personality and Social Psychology* 94, no. 2 (2008): 292–306.

Greene, Robert. *The 48 Laws of Power.* London: Profile Books, 2000.

Herbert, Steve. "Tangled Up in Blue: Conflicting Paths to Police Legitimacy." *Theoretical Criminology* 10, no. 4 (2006): 481–504.

Hetey, Rebecca C. and Jennifer L. Eberhardt. "Racial Disparities in Incarceration Increase Acceptance of Punitive Policies." *Psychological Science* 25, no. 10 (2014): 1949–54.

Hurwitz, Mark and Jon Peffley. *Justice in America: The Separate Realities of Blacks and Whites.* New York: Cambridge University Press, 2010.

Hyland, Shelley. *Police Use of Nonfatal Force.* Special Report, Washington, D.C.: Office of Justice Programs: The Bureau of Justice Statistics of the U.S. Department of Justice, 2002.

Ihlandfeldt, Keith and Benjamin Scafidi. "Whites' Neighborhood Racial Preferences and Neighborhood Racial Composition in the United States: Evidence from the Multi-City Study of Urban Inequality." *Housing Studies* 9, no. 3 (2004): 325–59.

Johnson, Kevin R. "How Racial Profiling in America Became the Law of the Land: United States v. Brignoni-Ponce and Whren v. United States and the Need for Truly Rebellious Lawyering." *Georgetown Law Journal* 98 (2010): 1005–77.

Jordan, Robert H. Jr. *Murder in the News: An Inside Look at How Television Covers Crime.* New York: Prometheus, 2017.

Kappeler, Victor E. *A Brief History of Slavery and the Origins of American Policing.* January 7, 2014. Accessed July 24, 2018. https://plsonline.eku .edu/insidelook/brief-history-slavery-and-origins-american-policing.

Krause, Don and Mark Smith. "Twitter as Mythmaker in Storytelling." *The Journal of Social Media in Society* 3 (2014): 8–27.

LaBarge, Scott. *Heroism: Why Heroes Are Important.* January 1, 2000. Accessed November 12, 2017. https://www.scu.edu/ethics/focus -areas/more/resources/heroism-why-heroes-are-important/.

Lai, Yun-Lien. *Policing Diversity: Determinants of White, Black, and Hispanic Attitudes Toward Police.* El Paso: LFB Scholarly Publishing, 2013.

Lawrence, Regina G. *The Politics of Force: Media and the Construction of Police Brutality.* Berkeley: University of California Press, 2000.

Lewandowski, Sierra. "The Color of Violence." *Academia* May 19, 2017. Accessed February 23, 2018. http://www.academia.edu/33407306 /The_Color_of_Violence.

Lockhart, P.R. "White People Keep Calling the Cops on Black People for No Reason. That's Dangerous." Vox. Accessed May 20, 2018. https:// www.vox.com/identities/2018/5/11/17340908/racial-profiling-star bucks-yale-police-violence-911-bias

Lum, Cynthia and Daniel S. Nagin. "Reinventing American Policing." *Crime and Justice* 46 (2017): 339–93.

Marcou, Dan. *10 Reasons Why American Police Officers Are Warriors.* July 12, 2016. Accessed June 7, 2017. https://www.policeone.com /police-heroes/articles/197073006-10-reasons-why-American-police -officers-are-warriors/.

Makarechi, Kia. "What the Data Really Says About Police and Racial Bias." Vanity Fair, https://www.vanityfair.com/news/2016/07/data-police -racial-bias. Accessed May 20, 2018.

Massey, Douglas. *Categorically Unequal: The American Stratification System.* New York: Russell Sage Foundation, 2007.

McNair, Ayana. *The Captive Public: Media Representations of the Police and the (Il)Legitimacy of Police Power.* Los Angeles: University of Southern California, 2011.

Mentel, Zoe. *Racial Reconciliation, Truth-Telling, and Police Legitimacy. Research Guide.* Washington, D.C.: U.S. Department of Justice: Office of Community Oriented Policing Services, 2012.

Muhammad, Khalil Gibran. *The Condemnation of Blackness: Race, Crime, and the Making of Modern Urban America.* Cambridge: Harvard University Press, 2010.

Natapoff, Alexandra. "Criminal Misdemeanor Theory and Practice." *Oxford Handbooks Online.* October 2016. Accessed May 21, 2018. http://www.oxfordhandbooks.com/view/10.1093/oxfordhb/97801999353 52.001.0001/oxfordhb-9780199935352-e-9.

Oliver, Mary Beth. "African American Men as 'Criminal and Dangerous': Implications of Media Portrayals of Crime on the 'Criminalization' of African American Men." *Journal of African American Studies* 7, no. 2 (2003): 3–18.

Owusu-Bempah, Akwasi. "Race and Policing in Historical Context: Dehumanization and the Policing of Black People in the 21st Century." *Theoretical Criminology* 21, no. 1 (2016): 23–34.

Peffley, Mark and Jon Hurwitz. *Justice in America: The Separate Realities of Blacks and Whites.* New York: Cambridge University Press, 2010.

Pelaez, Vicky. *Global Research: Center for Research on Globalization.* March 10, 2008. Accessed July 24, 2018. http://www.globalresearch .ca/the-prison-industry-in-the-united-states-big-business-or-a -new-form-of-slavery/8289.

Piquero, Kane, Meaghan Paulhamus, Robert J. Kane, and Alex R. Piquero. "State of the Science in Racial Profiling Research." In *Race, Ethnicity, and Policing: New and Essential Readings,* edited by Stephen K. Rice and Michael D. White, 239–58. New York: New York University Press, 2010.

Robinson, Cyril D. and Richard Scaglion. "The Origin and Evolution of the Police Function in Society: Notes Toward a Theory." *Law & Society Review* 21, no. 1 (1987): 109–31.

Sellin, Thorsten. "The Negro Criminal. A Statistical Note." *The Annals of the American Academy of Political and Social Science* 140 (1928): 52–64.

Snyder, Benjamin. *Policing the Police: Conflict Theory and Police Violence in a Racialized Society.* MA Thesis. Seattle: University of Washington, 2013.

Thompson, Victor R. and Lawrence D. Bobo. "Thinking about Crime: Race and Lay Accounts of Lawbreaking Behavior." *Digital Access to Scholarship at Harvard* October 27, 2013. Accessed July 3, 2018. http://nrs.harvard.edu/urn-3:HUL.InstRepos:11223561.

Tonry, Michael. *Punishing Race: A Continuing American Dilemma.* New York: Oxford University Press, 2011.

Travis, Jeremy. "Attitudes Toward Crime, Police, and the Law: Individual and Neighborhood Differences." *National Institute of Justice* June 1999. Accessed May 5, 2018. www.ncjrs.gov/pdffiles1/fs000240.pdf.

Voigta, Rob. "Language from Police Body Camera Footage Shows Racial Disparities in Officer Respect." *Proceedings of the National Academy of Sciences of the United States of America* 114, no. 25 (2017): 6521–26.

Way, Lori Beth and Ryan Patten. *Hunting for Dirtbags: Why Cops Over-Police the Poor and Racial Minorities.* Boston: Northeastern University Press, 2013.

Weitzer, Ronald and Steven A. Tuch. "Race, Class, and Perceptions of Discrimination by the Police." *Crime & Delinquency* 45, no. 4 (1999): 494–507.

Wilson, Jeremy M., Erin Dalton, Charles Scheer, and Clifford A. Grammich. *Police Recruitment and Retention for the New Millennium.* Santa Monica: RAND, 2010.

Zimbardo, Philip. *What Makes a Hero.* January 18, 2011. Accessed September 26, 2017. https://greatergood.berkeley.edu/article/item/what_makes _a_hero.

Index

About the Author

Terrell Carter, DMin, is a former police officer for the city of St. Louis, Missouri. During his tenure as an officer, he patrolled two of St. Louis's most dangerous districts as a uniformed patrolman and plainclothes narcotics investigator. Carter currently serves as vice president and chief diversity officer at Greenville University in Greenville, Illinois. Previously, he served as assistant professor and director of contextualized learning at Central Baptist Theological Seminary in Shawnee, Kansas.